"Vern Poythress's fine book argues a [t...] is as wide as creation and therefore as wide as our everyday activities. He shows how Jesus's saving works and Word apply to absolutely every sphere of life—to art and science, business and entrepreneurship, scholarship and education, politics and economics. Any Christian who wishes to honor the Lord Christ in the totality of his or her life should buy this book and read it immediately."

Bruce Riley Ashford, Provost and Associate Professor of Theology and Culture, Southeastern Baptist Theological Seminary

"Vern Poythress is one of the few writers today who combines rigorous scholarship and biblical theology with deep, practical spirituality. This volume is a defense of the notion, so powerfully expressed in the Reformed tradition in general and by Abraham Kuyper in particular, that Christ is Lord over every area of life. Building on this heritage, Poythress brings important clarifications along with practical applications not always found in the pioneers. Readers should not be deceived by the enviable simplicity of the arguments; they pack a wallop."

William Edgar, Professor of Apologetics, Westminster Theological Seminary

"My good friend Vern Poythress has written *Redeeming Science, Redeeming Sociology, Redeeming Mathematics,* and *Redeeming Philosophy,* as well as excellent books on linguistics and logic. *The Lordship of Christ* expounds the foundation beneath all these other studies—namely, the fact that Christ rules over every area of human life. This is the principle rediscovered by Abraham Kuyper, that every square inch in the universe belongs to Jesus. Poythress's book contains a strong biblical defense of this principle. It also contains the best discussion yet of the one-kingdom/two-kingdoms controversy."

John M. Frame, J. D. Trimble Chair of Systematic Theology and Philosophy, Reformed Theological Seminary, Orlando

"Thanks to Vern Poythress for providing an accessible, encouraging, practical study on the lordship of Christ. Any Christian who has questions about the authority of Christ and the joy of serving him will be greatly helped by this book. It revitalizes and reinvigorates a proper understanding of Christ the King. This book would be a useful tool for churches and Sunday school classes."

K. Scott Oliphint, Professor of Apologetics and Systematic Theology, Westminster Theological Seminary; author, *Covenantal Apologetics*

"For anyone looking for a clear, accessible, and biblically sound introduction to the kingship of Christ as understood in the Kuyperian strain of the Reformed tradition, this is the book that fills the bill. What makes the Kuyperian understanding of the kingdom so attractive to many is that it calls Christians to be active in every sphere of society and culture (not least the academy), and this book does an excellent job of illustrating the cultural claims of Christ's rule. At the same time, Poythress is careful to highlight some of the potential pitfalls of such an emphasis on Christian cultural engagement. One of the book's strengths is its liberal use of pertinent Bible texts to illustrate its points, without falling into facile proof-texting. An added bonus is that the book includes an extensive appendix in which the author enters into dialogue with the proponents of so-called 'two kingdoms' theology, where in a non-polemical way he points out some of the conceptual confusions that have too often bedeviled the discussion around this topic."

Albert M. Wolters, Professor Emeritus of Religion, Redeemer University College; author, *Creation Regained*

The Lordship of Christ

Other Crossway Books by Vern S. Poythress

Chance and the Sovereignty of God: A God-Centered Approach to Probability and Random Events

Inerrancy and the Gospels: A God-Centered Approach to the Challenges of Harmonization

Inerrancy and Worldview: Answering Modern Challenges to the Bible

In the Beginning Was the Word: Language—A God-Centered Approach

Logic: A God-Centered Approach to the Foundation of Western Thought

The Miracles of Jesus: How the Savior's Mighty Acts Serve as Signs of Redemption

Redeeming Mathematics: A God-Centered Approach

Redeeming Philosophy: A God-Centered Approach to the Big Questions

Redeeming Science: A God-Centered Approach

Redeeming Sociology: A God-Centered Approach

The Lordship of Christ

*Serving Our Savior All of the Time,
in All of Life, with All of Our Heart*

Vern S. Poythress

WHEATON, ILLINOIS

Trade paperback ISBN: 978-1-4335-4953-3
ePub ISBN: 978-1-4335-4956-4
PDF ISBN: 978-1-4335-4954-0
Mobipocket ISBN: 978-1-4335-4955-7

Library of Congress Cataloging-in-Publication Data

Names: Poythress, Vern S.
Title: The lordship of Christ : serving our Savior all of the time, in all of life, with all of our heart / Vern S. Poythress.
Description: Wheaton : Crossway, 2016. | Includes bibliographical references and index.
Identifiers: LCCN 2015036850 (print) | LCCN 2015032926 (ebook) | ISBN 9781433549540 (pdf) | ISBN 9781433549557 (mobi) | ISBN 9781433549564 (epub) | ISBN 9781433549533 (tp)
Subjects: LCSH: Service (Theology) | Christian life. | Jesus Christ—Lordship.
Classification: LCC BT738.4 (print) | LCC BT738.4 .P69 2016 (ebook) | DDC 248.4—dc23
LC record available at http://lccn.loc.gov/2015036850

Crossway is a publishing ministry of Good News Publishers.

CH   26   25   24   23   22   21   20   19   18   17   16
15   14   13   12   11   10   9   8   7   6   5   4   3   2   1

Contents

Part 1

THE CALL TO
SERVE CHRIST

1

Being Radically Christian

The Bible has a radical, earthshaking message about Jesus Christ. It says that Jesus Christ is not merely a human being, not merely a famous religious teacher, but the Lord of the universe. Matthew 28:18 includes this claim: "*All authority* in heaven and on earth has been given to me [Jesus]." Similarly, Ephesians 1:22 says, "He [God] put *all things* under his [Christ's] feet."

That message has profound implications for everyone living on the face of the earth. It has implications especially for what we think—for the life of the mind. It has implications not only for individuals but also for society. This book concentrates especially on these two points—implications for the mind and for society.

Implications for Society

How does the lordship of Christ have implications for society? In the modern West, many cultural leaders wish to keep religion private. They say, "Keep it to yourself," or "Keep it inside your family." Cultural leaders want most of life to be "secular," a realm where religion makes no difference. They say, in effect, "Keep your Jesus out of business, work, education, science, technology, government, politics, entertainment, media, and the arts." But if

Jesus is in fact Lord of all, he is Lord of all these areas of life. He is already there in his divine authority and power and presence. You cannot "keep him out." And trying to keep him out is already a violation of his claims to lordship.

IMPLICATIONS FOR NON-CHRISTIANS AND FOR CHRISTIANS

The message of the Bible has implications for all non-Christians, because Christ is Lord over each of their lives. Christ makes a claim on each human life. If he is Lord, he demands allegiance. He is not just someone you call in or consider if you think you need him. Nor is he someone who makes a claim only on Christians. His claim extends to everyone.

The lordship of Jesus Christ also has implications for everyone who is already a Christian believer. Many a person who claims to be a Christian drifts along without concerted attention to what it means to say that Jesus is Lord. A Christian may feel some kind of attachment to Jesus Christ but still not take seriously the radical changes that should take place with those who follow Christ.

WHO IS A CHRISTIAN?

Here we should observe that the word *Christian* in our day can be used quite loosely. There are people who consider themselves Christian because they live in the United States, and they suppose that the United States is a Christian nation (after all, it is not really Buddhist or Jewish or Muslim; only a small minority of US residents have these other religious commitments). Or they think they are Christian because their parents were Christian, or because they were once baptized, though they no longer believe much regarding the person of Christ. Then there are people who have some respect for Jesus Christ and who may read the Bible and go to church. But they still have not put their trust in Christ for salvation, and they do not have a personal relationship with God the Father and Christ his Son, established by the Holy Spirit.

In contrast to all these people, I have in mind born-again Christians, those who actually believe in Christ and follow him. But even the term *born-again* has its problems. People may think they are born again merely because they had an experience of religious excitement at some point, and they seemed for a while to feel differently about God and the world. Or they professed to make a commitment to Christ at some point, but their commitment was superficial and they did not really change.

That is not what the Bible means by being born again. Being born again is a radical change brought about by the Holy Spirit.

> Jesus answered him, "Truly, truly, I say to you, unless one is *born again* he cannot see the kingdom of God." (John 3:3)

> Jesus answered, "Truly, truly, I say to you, unless one is born of water and *the Spirit*, he cannot enter the kingdom of God. That which is born of the flesh is flesh, and that which is *born of the Spirit* is spirit. Do not marvel that I said to you, 'You must be born again.'" (John 3:5–7)

> For everyone who has been *born of God* overcomes the world. And this is the victory that has overcome the world—our faith. Who is it that overcomes the world except the one who believes that Jesus is the Son of God? (1 John 5:4–5)

> We know that everyone who has been *born of God* does not keep on sinning, but he [Jesus] who was born of God protects him, and the evil one does not touch him. (1 John 5:18)

Being born again involves being delivered from the power of evil and experiencing salvation.

RADICAL CHANGE

What happens when we acknowledge the lordship of Christ? Taking seriously the lordship of Christ involves radical change. Radical change can sound hard and unappealing. In some respects it is not only hard but impossible. At a fundamental level, we cannot change ourselves by our own power. But the good news of Christ includes the promise of his presence and his transforming power. "What is impossible with man is possible with God" (Luke 18:27). God delivers us from the invisible chains in life from which we could never deliver ourselves: "He has *delivered* us from the *domain* of darkness and transferred us to the *kingdom* of his beloved Son, in whom we have redemption, the forgiveness of sins" (Col. 1:13–14).

The fundamental problem is the problem of sin and guilt. "You were dead in the *trespasses and sins* in which you once walked" (Eph. 2:1–2). Only as we begin to see the magnitude of the problem do we give up following our own ways and making up our own rules and following our own desires.

One fundamental change is in our status before God. We change from being guilty to being forgiven. God is holy, and our sins have made us guilty before him. He created us and we owe everything to him. But we have broken his law and dishonored his name. We deserve death: "The wages of sin is death" (Rom. 6:23). Through Christ God promises to forgive our sins: "If we confess our sins, he is faithful and just to *forgive us our sins* and to cleanse us from all unrighteousness" (1 John 1:9). Christ bore the penalty for our sins, and we are counted righteous because of the righteousness of Christ (2 Cor. 5:21). "He himself bore our sins in his body on the tree, that we might die to sin and live to righteousness. By his wounds you have been healed" (1 Pet. 2:24).

The changes that God brings about include changes in the whole person: "If anyone is in Christ, he is a *new creation*" (2 Cor. 5:17). The fundamental change is as radical an event as being born, as we saw from John 3:3 and 3:5 above.

The changes include not only new beliefs but also new standards of judgment that we bring to the table when we are considering claims about truth. The changes include different behavior: we no longer try to make up our own moral standards but instead submit to the law of Christ our King. We receive power through the Spirit of Christ to begin to walk in the ways of Christ: "For those who live according to the flesh set their minds on the things of the flesh, but those who *live according to the Spirit* set their minds on the things of the Spirit" (Rom. 8:5).

The changes include transformed attitudes and motives. We grow in loving Christ and in experiencing his love for us. Out of that love, we grow in loving others: "*We love* because he first loved us" (1 John 4:19). We cast off hatred, jealousy, envy, selfish ambition (Gal. 5:19–21; Col. 3:5; James 3:14).

Change in the Mind

We also change in our thinking, in our minds: "Do not be conformed to this world, but be *transformed by the renewal of your mind*, that by testing you may *discern* what is the will of God, what is good and acceptable and perfect" (Rom. 12:2). This change in the mind takes place because the mercy of God has come to us, and we respond by devoting our whole selves to God: Thus, the apostle Paul writes, "I appeal to you therefore, brothers, by *the mercies of God*, to present your bodies as *a living sacrifice*, holy and acceptable to God, which is your spiritual worship" (Rom. 12:1). The change in our minds takes place as one aspect of a larger change, the transformation of the whole person. The Bible calls us to give complete submission to God in every aspect of life: we "present [our] bodies as a living sacrifice" (Rom. 12:1).

There are many good books providing Christians with resources for growing in their faith.[1] We need to start at the beginning, by hearing the good news of what Christ has achieved in his death and resurrection. We not only need to hear but also need to believe in Christ. God works in us through the Holy Spirit so that we trust in Christ and in the salvation that he has accomplished.

We continue in the same way we have begun, by trusting in Christ. The most fundamental way of growing is through the

---

[1] I recommend J. I. Packer, *Knowing God* (Downers Grove, IL: InterVarsity Press, 1993), as one good starting point.

means that God himself has provided, sometimes called "the means of grace." The means include reading and studying the Bible, listening to the Word of God preached, praying, participating in the sacraments (baptism and the Lord's Supper), and having fellowship with believers in the body of Christ. When used by the Holy Spirit, these means bring about change in the whole person.

RESISTANCE FROM A SECULAR SOCIETY

In our environment, Christians do not always include in their idea of change the particular kind of change mentioned in Romans 12:2, the renewal of the mind. Change in behavior, yes. Change in attitudes by growing in love, yes. Change in beliefs, yes—at least when a person initially becomes a follower of Christ. But what about change in the mind? Christians do not always think about that area.

As we have observed, the surrounding culture in modern Western countries does *not* encourage us to think about such changes. Cultural leaders want most of life to be secular. According to this view, most of your thinking about business, work, education, and so on is supposed to be the same as everyone else's. Christianity makes a difference only in private, or only when you are in a church building during a worship service. In this picture only small pieces of life are influenced by the presence of Christ.

Such a view is very different from the Bible's principle that Christ is Lord of everything and that our minds are to be transformed and renewed by his presence. It is also notably different from past centuries in Europe, when Christian principles had wider influence on society, showing their effects in law, art, music, science, and many social organizations.

Being radically Christian means no longer naively accepting the cultural message of secularity. We belong to Christ. Christ is Lord not merely over individual souls but over the universe.

As the message about Jesus Christ goes out to the world, God is commanding everyone to repent and come to Christ: "The times of ignorance God overlooked, but now he *commands all people* everywhere to repent, because he has fixed a day on which he will judge the world in righteousness by a man whom he has appointed; and of this he has given assurance to all by raising him from the dead" (Acts 17:30–31). Coming to Christ in faith involves acknowledging that he is the universal Master and Lord: "If you confess with your mouth that Jesus is *Lord* and believe in your heart that God raised him from the dead, you will be saved. For with the heart one believes and is justified, and with the mouth one confesses and is saved" (Rom. 10:9–10).

The Call to Service

What are the implications? Over a century ago, Abraham Kuyper grasped the implications and made a ringing announcement: "No single piece of our mental world is to be hermetically sealed off from the rest, and there is not a square inch in the whole domain of our human existence over which Christ, who is Sovereign over *all*, does not cry: 'Mine!'"[2] In this book we will be exploring the implications of the fact that Christ is indeed "Sovereign over *all.*"

As we explore these implications, we should keep clear what is the basis for our salvation. We are saved by the work of Christ on the cross, not by our own good works. When we strive to obey Christ, we do *not* do so because our works earn salvation for us. They could never be good enough for that. We serve Christ because we have *already* been saved, by grace alone. We respond in gratitude because we have come to love Christ. Christ has changed us, both by wiping away our guilt and by renewing our hearts.

We could, if we wish, jump right into a discussion of what Christ's lordship means for politics, science, education, and other

---

[2] Abraham Kuyper, "Sphere Sovereignty," in *Abraham Kuyper: A Centennial Reader*, ed. James D. Bratt (Grand Rapids, MI: Eerdmans, 1998), 488, italics original. The quote was originally part of Kuyper's speech at the inauguration of the Free University of Amsterdam in 1880. Kuyper's declaration about Christ's lordship can be seen as exemplifying the biblical theme of exclusive loyalty to God (Ex. 20:3; 1 Kings 18:21). This quote and the larger context of the life of Abraham Kuyper influenced a recent book on the topic: Bruce Riley Ashford, *Every Square Inch: An Introduction to Cultural Engagement for Christians* (Bellingham, WA: Lexham, 2015); see Ashford's comment on p. 6.

areas of modern life. We will get to all that in part 3 of this book. But it is important that we not be too hasty. The transformation of life includes transformation of how we think about the challenge of radical change itself. What are the proper foundations for Christian living? And what are the resources for serving Christ? These questions deserve our attention here in part 1 and then in part 2 respectively.

2

The Story of Redemption

If we are going to think through the life of the mind in the most radical way, we must do it in the context of the complete picture given in the Bible. The Bible indicates that we live within a world created by God, in a history governed by God, as human beings responsible to God. The view of the world presented in Scripture is deeply at odds with the typical thinking of "modern man," the person who wants to break free of God and live in a secular world. It is appropriate, therefore, to review briefly the basic elements belonging to a biblical view of the world.

What Is Wrong

The Bible has a message about what is wrong with the world and what is the fundamental answer to this wrong. This message involves Christ at its center. Through Christ, and him alone, human beings can have their sins forgiven and be reconciled to God. Christ is the one Mediator between God and man, through whom the alienation between God and man is overcome.

> For there is one God, and there is *one mediator* between God and men, *the man Christ Jesus*, who gave himself as a ransom for all. (1 Tim. 2:5–6)

And there is salvation *in no one else*, for there is no other name under heaven given among men by which we must be saved. (Acts 4:12)

Jesus said to him, "I am *the way*, and the truth, and the life. No one comes to the Father except through me." (John 14:6)

The Message in Context

This is the message of Christianity—that is, the message of Christianity properly understood. It is the message found in the Bible. And it is the message that was proclaimed by the followers of Christ in the first centuries after Christ's resurrection from the dead. But in our day there is much confusion. Many people say many things in the name of Christianity and in the name of Christ. And many people have done good deeds in the name of Christ. But others have done evil while invoking his name. So it is important that we return to the Bible and discover the real truth about Christ and his claims.

The History of Redemption

The truths about Christ make sense only when we see them in the context of the full teaching of the Bible.[1] The Bible begins not with Christ the Redeemer but with the creation of the world: "In the beginning, God created the heavens and the earth" (Gen. 1:1).

This teaching by itself is incredibly radical, because it affirms the presence of God and his unique character in relation to the world. We do not live in a meaningless world of mere matter and motion, as a materialist philosophy would have us believe. We live in God's world, a world that he not only created but continues to rule over. In most of this book I talk about the lordship of Christ, but even that truth should be seen in the context of the full biblical teaching about God. God is one God in three persons—

---

[1] D. A. Carson, *Christ and Culture Revisited* (Grand Rapids, MI: Eerdmans, 2008), 44–65, expands on my short summary and helpfully points to many implications for our understanding of the relation of Christians to "culture." The book is in many respects complementary to mine.

the Father, the Son, and the Holy Spirit. Honoring Christ the Son of God goes together with honoring God in his fullness. We honor all three persons together. If we are serving and obeying Christ the Lord, we are simultaneously serving God the Father and the Holy Spirit.

As a central part of his work in creating the world, God created man in his image.

> So God created man *in his own image*,
> in the *image of God* he created him;
> male and female he created them. (Gen. 1:27)

We are responsible to God as his creatures, especially made as persons who can enjoy a personal relation with him. We are responsible to receive his love and return love to him.

Adam, the first man, disobeyed God's command and fell into a state of rebellion against God (Gen. 3:6–7). The human race has been living in rebellion ever since. Through the generations, God showed mercy to the human race and made promises concerning the coming of Christ as Redeemer.

In the fullness of time, Christ came to earth and proclaimed a message of deliverance. Then, in accordance with God's plan, he died to bear the penalty of sins and was raised to new life on the third day to bring new life and forgiveness to those who trust in him: "[He] was delivered up for our trespasses and raised for our justification" (Rom. 4:25).

We wait for the time when he will come again and bring a new heaven and a new earth, completely free from sin and death and the corruptions of this world (Rev. 21:1–4).

In sum, the Bible gives us several major points about God and the history of the world:

- *God*. God always existed. He is one God in three persons.
- *Creation*. The world came into existence when God created it.

- *Fall.* Adam rebelled against God and engulfed the human race in sin.
- *Redemption.* Christ came from the Father and accomplished redemption by his crucifixion and resurrection from the dead.
- *Consummation.* Christ has promised to return, and God will create a new heaven and a new earth.

Further Points of Importance

We could describe this history given to us in the Bible in much greater detail. But we will content ourselves with a few further points.

The Lordship of Christ as God and Man

First, the language about Christ's lordship involves the full person of Christ, who is God and man. Ever since his incarnation, Christ has been both God and man. He is God from all eternity: "In the beginning was the Word, and the Word was with God, and the Word was God" (John 1:1). He became man through the virgin conception of Mary: "And the Word *became flesh* and dwelt among us" (John 1:14).

When Romans 10:9 says that "Jesus is *Lord*," it implies that he is God. We can see this by noting that one of the neighboring verses, Romans 10:13, uses the same word *Lord* (*kurios* in Greek) in a quotation taken from Joel 2:32. Translated "Lord" in verse 32, the word represents the special name of the God of Israel, the four-letter Hebrew name that the Jews regarded as most sacred of all, the name that occurs also in Exodus 3:14–15:

> God said to Moses, "I am who I am." And he said, "Say this to the people of Israel, 'I am has sent me to you.'" God also said to Moses, "Say this to the people of Israel, 'The Lord, the God of your fathers, the God of Abraham, the God of Isaac, and the God of Jacob, has sent me to you.' This is my name forever, and thus I am to be remembered throughout all generations."

To confess Jesus to be Lord is to confess him to be God, the same God who is the God of Israel and who created the world. Jesus is therefore worthy of absolute allegiance. In giving allegiance to Jesus we are at the same time giving allegiance to God the Father and God the Holy Spirit, because the three persons are one God.

In addition, we ascribe the name *Lord* to Jesus because he has been exalted as a reward for his obedient suffering.

> And being found in human form, he humbled himself by becoming obedient to the point of death, even death on a cross. Therefore God has *highly exalted him* and bestowed on him the name that is above every name, so that at the name of Jesus every knee should bow, in heaven and on earth and under the earth, and every tongue confess that Jesus Christ is *Lord*, to the glory of God the Father. (Phil. 2:8–11)

Jesus always has been God. He is also fully man since the time of his incarnation. He suffered and died and then was exalted. These latter descriptions apply to his human nature. His exaltation gives him full authority over all things.

> And Jesus came and said to them, "*All authority* in heaven and on earth has been given to me." (Matt. 28:18)

> . . . according to the working of his great might that he [God] worked in Christ when he raised him from the dead and *seated him at his right hand* in the heavenly places, far above all rule and authority and power and dominion, and above every name that is named, not only in this age but also in the one to come. And he put *all things* under his feet and gave him as *head over all things* to the church, which is his body, the fullness of him who fills all in all. (Eph. 1:19–23)

Christ our Redeemer has a special relation of love to those who belong to him and to his body, the church. But the verses in Ephesians 1:19–23 do not say that he is Lord *only* over the church.

He is "head over *all things*" (v. 22). He is given *to the church*, "which is his body" (v. 23).

Christ rules over all things because he is God. As God, he exercises his rule from creation onward to the consummation, and beyond. But it is also true that he rules over all things because he is exalted through his resurrection and ascension. This exaltation is the way in which God fulfills his design for mankind to have dominion.

> So God created man in his own image,
>   in the image of God he created him;
>   male and female he created them.

> And God blessed them. And God said to them, "Be fruitful and multiply and fill the earth and subdue it, and *have dominion* over the fish of the sea and over the birds of the heavens and over every living thing that moves on the earth." (Gen. 1:27–28)

Later parts of the Bible take up this same language of human dominion, as we can see in Psalms 8 and 110:

> You have given him [man] *dominion* over the works of
>   your hands;
>   you have *put all things under his feet*,
> all sheep and oxen,
>   and also the beasts of the field. (Ps. 8:6–7)

> The LORD says to my Lord:
>   "Sit at my right hand,
> until I make your enemies *your footstool*." (Ps. 110:1)

This divine plan for human dominion is fulfilled in Christ, as is illustrated by the expression "put all things under his feet" in Ephesians 1:22. Another passage, Hebrews 2:6–9, confirms this idea by directly applying the words of Psalm 8 to Jesus. While Psalm 8 is focusing on dominion given to mankind, Hebrews 2:9

applies these truths to Jesus. It is Jesus who in his human nature has brought about the fulfillment of God's task of dominion given to mankind.[2]

Thus, Christ rules over all things as God and man. His divine nature and human nature belong together, because the two natures are united in one person. The *person* of Christ is ruling over all.

THE FIRST AND THE LAST ADAM

Second, Christ's work has a close connection with the work of Adam. Hebrews 2:6–9 implies that Christ has fulfilled the task of dominion originally given to Adam. Adam failed, through his sin. By contrast, Christ did not fail but achieved the victory. Adam was head and representative over all humanity, which descended from him. We inherit sin and death from him. Christ is head and representative over the *new* humanity, which consists in the church, the company of the redeemed. Through him, all who believe in him inherit his perfect righteousness and his Adamic achievement; we inherit eternal life and the new world to come, the new heaven and the new earth. The parallel between Adam and Christ is expounded at some length in Romans 5:12–21 and 1 Corinthians 15:20–26, 45–49. Christ is called "the last Adam" in 1 Corinthians 15:45 to indicate the parallel between him and the first Adam.

TWO STAGES IN CHRIST'S DOMINION AND REDEMPTION

Third, the New Testament indicates that the redemption that Christ achieved in his crucifixion and resurrection comes into effect in two stages. The first stage begins with Christ's resurrection and ascension. As Ephesians 1:22 indicates, God has already, at the time of his resurrection, "put all things under his feet." Christ rules over all. But he has not yet completely abolished sin and death. First Corinthians 15:26 indicates that "the last enemy to be

---

[2] Dan McCartney, "Ecce Homo: The Coming of the Kingdom as the Restoration of Human Vicegerency," *Westminster Theological Journal* 56, no. 1 (1994): 1–21.

destroyed is death." This event takes place at the second coming of Christ, when people are raised from the dead.

The New Testament indicates likewise that the believers' inheritance comes in two stages. During this age we have the gift of the Holy Spirit, who is the "guarantee" or "down payment" of our inheritance (Eph. 1:14; the ESV margin has "down payment"). We come into full possession of it when Christ returns. Our inheritance is already guaranteed by Christ (1 Pet. 1:3–4). We do not depend on our good works in order to earn it.

The New Testament also speaks of our adoption as sons as coming in two stages. We are adopted sons now because we are united to Christ: "So you are no longer a slave, but *a son*, and if a son, then *an heir* through God" (Gal. 4:7). Another place speaks of adoption coming in the future, at the time of Christ's coming: "And not only the creation, but we ourselves, who have the firstfruits of the Spirit, groan inwardly as we *wait eagerly for adoption as sons*, the redemption of our bodies" (Rom. 8:23).

The two sides are not really in tension, because our present adoption is real and at the same time is a foretaste or down payment of the future adoption. These two stages belong together because both are the work of Christ, based on his Adamic achievement of obedience and the reward that he received in his resurrection. He ascended to heaven and now sits at the right hand of God, the place from which he rules over all things.

The Gift of the Holy Spirit

Fourth, the Holy Spirit comes as the fruit of Christ's exaltation. When Christ was raised from the dead, he was exalted to the right hand of God: "This Jesus God raised up, and of that we all are witnesses. Being therefore *exalted at the right hand of God*, and having received from the Father the promise of the Holy Spirit, he has poured out this that you yourselves are seeing and hearing" (Acts 2:32–33).

As a result of Christ's exaltation, he poured out the Holy Spirit

on the church in the day of Pentecost (Acts 2:1–4). The Holy
Spirit is the Spirit of Christ, who dwells in those who believe in
him (Rom. 8:9–11). Through the Holy Spirit the resurrection
power of Christ is at work in us. Only through *his* power do
we receive the power to change in a fundamental way—to turn
from darkness to light and to walk as participants in the new
creation in Christ: "If anyone is in Christ, he is a *new creation*"
(2 Cor. 5:17).

As we live in Christ and in the power of the Holy Spirit, we
are not *supplementing* the work of Christ, as if his work were
incomplete. Rather, we are living out of the very energy of his
resurrection life. We began this new life when we were first spiritually united to Christ at the time of our conversion. We died to
the old life dominated by sin, and we were raised to new life: "If
then you have been raised with Christ . . ." (Col. 3:1). But it is also
true that the death and resurrection of Christ are being applied to
our lives every day.

> For we who live are *always* being given over to *death* for Jesus'
> sake, so that the *life* of Jesus also may be manifested in our
> mortal flesh. So *death* is at work in us, but *life* in you. (2 Cor.
> 4:11–12)

> . . . that I may know him and the power of his *resurrection*,
> and may share his sufferings, becoming like him in his *death*,
> that by any means possible I may attain the *resurrection* from
> the dead. (Phil. 3:10–11)

Christian living involves daily dying to selfishness and pride. And
daily we are being renewed by his resurrection, living in the power
of Christ and in the service of Christ.

We are living on the basis of his perfection and his achievement. But that also implies that we rule with him: "[God] raised
us up with him and *seated us with him* in the heavenly places in
Christ Jesus" (Eph. 2:6). This rule on the part of believers derives

from Christ's rule as the last Adam. Believers rule because they are united with Christ who rules. This rule is an exercise of *dominion*, a dominion in union with Christ. In some respects, it is comparable to what Adam failed to achieve when he rebelled against God. But it is better than Adam's dominion, because Christ as the last Adam surpasses even what Adam could have done. His rule is over the whole universe, not merely over the earth and the animals. He has eternal, resurrection life, not merely the ordinary, earthly life with which Adam began.

Thus, believers have a task of ruling. But they can do it only as they are empowered by Christ, and only on the basis of Christ's complete victory.

The Authority of Scripture

Fifth, the lordship of Christ implies the authority of Scripture. During his earthly life, Jesus affirmed the divine authority of the Old Testament. The Old Testament is the very word of God. We can see this implication from several of his statements:

> Do not think that I have come to abolish the Law or the Prophets; I have not come to abolish them but to *fulfill them*. For truly, I say to you, until heaven and earth pass away, not an iota, not a dot, will pass from the Law until all is accomplished. (Matt. 5:17–18)

> *Scripture* cannot be broken. (John 10:35)

> He [Jesus] answered, "Have you not read that *he who created them* from the beginning made them male and female, and said, 'Therefore a man shall leave his father and his mother and hold fast to his wife, and the two shall become one flesh'?" (Matt. 19:4–5)

The last of these sayings, from Matthew 19:4–5, is quite significant because Jesus quotes from Genesis 2:24, which is just a part of the normal narrative of Genesis. Yet Jesus identifies the speaker as "he who created them from the beginning," that is, God himself. This identification shows that Genesis 2:24 is God's word. By implication, the whole of Genesis is God's word.

We are obliged to accept the authority of Christ because he is God and is Lord of all. God is completely truthful and completely wise. When we accept his authority, we accept his teaching. And one aspect of his teaching is the affirmation of the divine authority of the Old Testament. The same authority belongs to the New Testament as well, because Christ commissioned his apostles with his authority.[3]

If Christ is our Master and we are his servants, we must obey him. But obedience means little or nothing unless there are specific *ways* that we must obey. We must avoid just making things up out of our own minds and declaring to ourselves that we are obedient. If we do this, we are replacing the real Christ described in Scripture with our own idea of Christ. We are fooling ourselves and others by saying that *our* ideas of Christ are what he really wants.

By contrast to this route of making up our own kind of "obedience," we have access to specific commandments of Christ and specific instructions from Christ in the Bible. The whole Bible is the word of God, and God is Father, Son, and Holy Spirit. The whole Bible is the word of Christ. So it is all relevant to us.

The Bible includes specific commandments. But it gives these commandments within a larger context of instruction, including instruction about the history of redemption. The larger context helps to guide our understanding. Moreover, we need wisdom in order to discern the implications for our lives. This wisdom comes from Christ.

---

[3] For detailed discussion of the authority of Scripture, see John Murray, "The Attestation of Scripture," in *The Infallible Word: A Symposium by Members of the Faculty of Westminster Theological Seminary*, ed. N. B. Stonehouse and Paul Woolley, 3rd ed. (Philadelphia: Presbyterian and Reformed, 1967), 1–54. The other chapters in the same volume are also valuable. On the New Testament canon, see Michael J. Kruger, *Canon Revisited: Establishing the Origins and Authority of the New Testament Books* (Wheaton, IL: Crossway, 2012).

And because of him [God] you are in Christ Jesus, who became to us *wisdom* from God, righteousness and sanctification and redemption. (1 Cor. 1:30)

. . . Christ, in whom are hidden all the treasures of *wisdom* and knowledge. (Col. 2:2–3)

The Bible needs to be interpreted. Not everything is equally easy to understand or apply. But our obedience to Christ is robust only if we receive the Bible with the submission that it deserves: we receive it as the word of God, the very speech of God, because that is what it is. Throughout our discussions, we will use the Bible as our infallible guide.

3

Reasons for Obedience to Christ

Why should we endeavor to obey Christ comprehensively? Why should we serve him in every area of life? There are many reasons. I will mention only a few.

Christ Is Universal Lord

The first and most obvious reason is the one that I have already discussed, namely, that Christ is universal Lord. If he is Lord of all, he is Lord over business and work and education and science and home life. The business owner is not an absolute owner but a subordinate owner, a steward. God owns all things. He has given gifts to human beings, as a trust. We are managers of God's estate, so to speak. This also means we are managers of Christ's estate, since he is God and, as man, he has inherited the world: "but in these last days he has spoken to us by his Son, whom he appointed the *heir of all things*" (Heb. 1:2). Each worker is to be working at the tasks assigned to him by the Lord, within the context of God's providence: "He upholds *the universe* by the word of his power" (Heb. 1:3).

The obligation to serve Christ is even more obvious when applied to Christians. Genuine Christians are those who have trusted in Christ. Because of that trust, they have submitted themselves to his lordship. They have confessed that "Jesus is Lord" (Rom. 10:9). Consequently, they are "servants" of Christ or "slaves" of Christ:

Paul, a *servant* [or slave] of Christ Jesus . . . (Rom. 1:1)

he who was free when called is a *bondservant* [or slave] of Christ. (1 Cor. 7:22)

The key word in Greek for servant or bondservant or slave is *doulos*. In its ordinary use in the Roman Empire, it describes those who were legally bound to serve their masters until their release.

Of course, with a human master the position of being bound to serve could be onerous. Servants suffered under oppressive masters. By contrast, Christ's lordship is entirely good. His servants can and should delight to serve him.

We need to consider seriously the depth of obligation involved. When anyone becomes a follower of Christ, he gives up his own life completely.

Now great crowds accompanied him, and he turned and said to them, "If anyone comes to me and does not hate his own father and mother and wife and children and brothers and sisters, yes, and *even his own life*, he cannot be my disciple. Whoever does not bear his own cross and come after me cannot be my disciple. For which of you, desiring to build a tower, does not first sit down and count the cost, whether he has enough to complete it? Otherwise, when he has laid a foundation and is not able to finish, all who see it begin to mock him, saying, 'This man began to build and was not able to finish.' Or what king, going out to encounter another king in war, will not sit down first and deliberate whether he is able with ten thousand to meet him who comes against him with twenty thousand? And if not, while the other is yet a great way off, he sends a delegation and asks for terms of peace. So therefore, any one of you who does not *renounce all that he has* cannot be my disciple." (Luke 14:25–33)

He no longer has a life "of his own." He is never off duty: "So you also, when you have done all that you were commanded, say, 'We are unworthy servants; we have *only* done what was *our duty*'" (Luke 17:10).

The follower of Christ must be a follower *all the time*.[1] Of course the meeting in church on Sunday is particularly important. We meet to celebrate the Lord's goodness, to hear his Word, to meditate on his character, to give thanks to him, to confess our sins, to receive forgiveness, to receive his power through the Holy Spirit, and to recommit ourselves to serving him. But our service to the Lord continues all week long. The Christian who works during the week is serving Christ.

> Bondservants, obey in everything those who are your earthly masters, not by way of eye-service, as people-pleasers, but with sincerity of heart, fearing the Lord. *Whatever you do*, work heartily, as *for the Lord* and not for men, knowing that from the Lord you will receive the inheritance as your reward. You are *serving the Lord Christ*. (Col. 3:22–24)

This passage in Colossians is directed specifically to those who are "bondservants," that is, slaves within the context of Roman society. They have no choice as to what kind of work they will do or whom they will serve. They have to serve their earthly master. God says that they are to serve *the Lord*, not *merely* an earthly master. They are to serve "with sincerity of heart," to "work heartily, as for the Lord." If this is true for bondservants, how much more should it be true for people who have more choice and control over what kind of work they do.

---

[1] "*Christians are Christian seven days a week*" (David VanDrunen, *Living in God's Two Kingdoms: A Biblical Vision for Christianity and Culture* [Wheaton, IL: Crossway, 2010], 162, italics original).

The Worthiness of Christ

Another reason for service to Christ is that Jesus Christ is worthy of praise and service. As a person, he is altogether lovely. But not everyone recognizes this loveliness. Isaiah 53:2 reminds us that during Christ's time on earth he did not attract people by earthly beauty:

> He had no form of majesty that we should look at him,
>   and *no beauty* that we should desire him.

In fact, he was despised.

> He was *despised* and rejected by men;
>   a man of sorrows, and acquainted with grief;
> and as one from whom men hide their faces
>   he was *despised*, and we esteemed him not. (Isa. 53:3)

Precisely when he was despised, he showed himself altogether worthy. Through the magnitude of his love and sacrifice on the cross he draws us to himself: "'And I, when I am lifted up from the earth, will *draw all people to myself.*' He said this to show by what kind of death he was going to die" (John 12:32–33).

Love for Christ

Another reason for service is that we love Jesus Christ. "*We love* because he first loved us" (1 John 4:19). Jesus says, "If you love me, you will keep my commandments" (John 14:15). Loving Christ is a form of loving God, as described in "the great and first commandment": "You shall *love the Lord your God* with all your heart and with all your soul and with all your mind. This is the great and first commandment" (Matt. 22:37–38).

In these verses Jesus repeats a central commandment given in the Old Testament law in Deuteronomy 6:5. In both the Old Testament and the New, the commandment is comprehensive in its reach and its intensity. Love is to be "with *all* your heart and with

all your soul and with *all* your might" (Deut. 6:5). This comprehensive reach is reinforced by the first commandment within the
Ten Commandments: "You shall have no other gods before me"
(Ex. 20:3). God deserves our complete allegiance. We are not to
divide it with anything or anyone else. The second commandment
reminds us of this same commitment by saying that God is a "jeal-
ous" God, who does not tolerate idolatry (Ex. 20:5).

If we love God, we should love him comprehensively, and we
should love him at every moment. Consequently, we should serve
him at every moment.

All this language can sound burdensome to people who desire
autonomy. But it is not burdensome in and of itself. God is worthy
of love. He is supremely lovely. And Christ, the only Son of God, is
supremely lovely. He has shown his love in saving us and justifying
us by his grace. We respond in gratitude for his love.

> God shows *his love* for us in that while we were still sinners,
> Christ died for us. (Rom. 5:8)

> He who did not spare his own Son but *gave him up for us all*,
> how will he not also with him graciously give us all things?
> (Rom. 8:32)

> Beloved, let us love one another, for *love is from God*, and
> whoever loves has been born of God and knows God. Anyone
> who does not love does not know God, because God is love.
> In this the love of God was made manifest among us, that God
> sent his only Son into the world, so that we might live through
> him. In this is love, not that we have loved God but that he
> loved us and sent his Son to be the propitiation for our sins.
> Beloved, if *God so loved us*, we also ought to love one another.
> No one has ever seen God; if we love one another, God abides
> in us and his love is perfected in us. (1 John 4:7–12)

In addition to all this, Christ has promised to be present with
us. He is present through the Holy Spirit, whom he has given us.

Through his presence he transforms us and empowers us for continual service.

> . . . teaching them to observe all that I have commanded you. And behold, *I am with you always*, to the end of the age. (Matt. 28:20)

> God's *love* has been poured into our hearts through the Holy Spirit *who has been given to us*. (Rom. 5:5)

> And we all, with unveiled face, beholding the glory of the Lord, are being *transformed* into the same image from one degree of glory to another. For this comes *from the Lord* who is the *Spirit*. (2 Cor. 3:18)

Our love does not become perfect within this life. We still fall into sins. But Christ offers forgiveness when we confess our sins (1 John 1:9).

Serving Christ Is Serving God

It is worthwhile reiterating the truth about the Trinitarian character of God. In serving Christ, we are serving God the Son, who is one with the Father and the Spirit. We are serving God, which is what we were created and designed to do.

The Joy of Serving Christ

Discussions of people's duty sometimes sound burdensome. But, according to Scripture, our duty is not burdensome when we are in fellowship with Christ.

> For this is the love of God, that we keep his commandments. And his commandments are not *burdensome*. For everyone who has been born of God overcomes the world. And this is the victory that has overcome the world—our faith. Who is it that overcomes the world except the one who believes that Jesus is the Son of God? (1 John 5:3–5)

Jesus promises us joy in serving him: "These things I have spoken to you, that my *joy* may be in you, and that your *joy* may be full. This is my commandment, that you love one another as I have loved you" (John 15:11–12). To outsiders looking at Christian discipleship, it can seem like we are sacrificing everything and giving up any prospect of happiness. The mystery of service is that, in giving up everything, we receive everything that matters.

> Whoever seeks to *preserve* his life will *lose* it, but whoever *loses* his life will *keep* it. (Luke 17:33)

> Whoever loves his life *loses* it, and whoever hates his life in this world will keep it for *eternal life*. If anyone serves me, he must follow me; and where I am, there will my servant be also. If anyone serves me, the Father will *honor him*. (John 12:25–26)

> For what will it profit a man if he *gains* the whole world and *forfeits* his soul? Or what shall a man give in return for his soul? (Matt. 16:26)

Christ Is All-Wise

We also serve Jesus Christ because he is all-wise. He is full of the very wisdom of God, as it says in Colossians 2:2–3: ". . . Christ, in whom are hidden all the treasures of *wisdom* and knowledge." So following him is the only wise way to live. We flourish as human beings when we follow God's way, not our own inventions.

The Glory of God

In addition, God has made the whole world to be a theater to display his glory. We ourselves, as creatures made in the image of God, are created to receive his glory and reflect it. We find our deepest satisfaction and the deepest fulfillment of who we are— who we were created to be—when we serve God: "Man's chief end is to glorify God, and to enjoy him forever."[2] In everything we do, we are to be animated by the goal of giving him glory.

> And I saw no temple in the city [the New Jerusalem], for its temple is the Lord God the Almighty and the Lamb. And the city has no need of sun or moon to shine on it, for *the glory of God* gives it light, and its lamp is the Lamb. (Rev. 21:22–23; see also 21:11)

> So, whether you eat or drink, or whatever you do, do all to *the glory of God.* (1 Cor. 10:31)

Fulfillment

As mentioned above, we find true fulfillment only when we are doing what we were created to do. The Bible does not promise that in this world we will be free from struggles and trials.

> When they had preached the gospel to that city and had made many disciples, they returned to Lystra and to Iconium and to Antioch, strengthening the souls of the disciples, encouraging them to continue in the faith, and saying that *through many tribulations* we must enter the kingdom of God. (Acts 14:21–22)

> For when we were with you, we kept telling you beforehand that we were to *suffer affliction*, just as it has come to pass, and just as you know. (1 Thess. 3:4)

Yet Jesus gives us unspeakable joy even in the midst of the tribulations.

> In this *you rejoice*, though now for a little while, if necessary, you have been grieved by various trials, so that the tested genuineness of your faith—more precious than gold that perishes though it is tested by fire—may be found to result in praise and glory and honor at the revelation of Jesus Christ. Though you

---

[2] Westminster Shorter Catechism, answer 1.

have not seen him, you love him. Though you do not now see
him, you believe in him and rejoice with *joy* that is inexpress-
ible and filled with glory. (1 Pet. 1:6–8)

I have said these things to you, that in me you may have *peace*.
In the world you will have *tribulation*. But take heart; I have
overcome the world. (John 16:33)

Fear of Hell

It is not popular in modern societies to talk about hell and the
fear of hell. But popularity does not change the truth. Hell exists.
Jesus warned people to repent and come to God, lest they suffer
eternal punishment:

The Son of Man will send his angels, and they will gather
out of his kingdom all causes of sin and all law-breakers, and
throw them into the fiery furnace. In that place there will be
weeping and gnashing of teeth. Then the righteous will shine
like the sun in the kingdom of their Father. (Matt. 13:41–43)

It is legitimate to speak the truth and to warn people about the solemn consequences of rebelling against God and against his Christ.
We ought to come to Jesus and submit to him because the alternative is to suffer in hell.

Multiple Motivations Lead to Serving God

Together, these various reasons coalesce in one direction—to motivate us, empower us, and command us to serve God in Christ.

Masters, do the same to them, and stop your threatening,
knowing that he who is both *their Master and yours* is in
heaven. (Eph. 6:9)

You are *serving the Lord Christ*. (Col. 3:24)

These principles can be classified according to John Frame's
three perspectives on ethics: the normative perspective, the

existential perspective, and the situational perspective.[3] The normative perspective focuses on the *norms* for our action. In this case, the norm is the authority of Christ as universal Lord. The existential perspective focuses on the person and on motivations. The motivation in this case is love for Christ. Finally, the situational perspective focuses on the situation and asks what will best promote the glory of God, which is the supreme goal in every situation. These perspectives interlock with one another and reinforce one another when properly used. Together they show how the purpose of God comes to bear on the lives of Christians, those who are followers of Christ.

The presence of Christ is related to all three perspectives. He is present as the *Lord*, who directs us and supplies *norms*. He is present with us in our *situation*. His presence motivates and empowers us, and thus affects our motives, our *existential* attitude.

---

[3] John M. Frame, *Perspectives on the Word of God: An Introduction to Christian Ethics* (Eugene, OR: Wipf & Stock, 1999); Frame, *The Doctrine of the Christian Life* (Phillipsburg, NJ: P&R, 2008).

4

Serving Christ in Our Knowledge

Christ is Lord of all. So he is Lord also in the area of knowledge and the standards for knowledge. Let us think about the implications.

Christ as Our Wisdom

Christ is the Lord of knowledge because he has all wisdom. This possession of wisdom—wisdom on our behalf—is evident in a number of passages:

> She [the queen of Sheba] came from the ends of the earth to hear the *wisdom* of Solomon, and behold, something *greater than Solomon* is here. (Matt. 12:42)

> And because of him you are in Christ Jesus, who became to us *wisdom* from God, righteousness and sanctification and redemption. (1 Cor. 1:30)

> . . . Christ, in whom are hidden *all the treasures of wisdom and knowledge*. (Col. 2:2–3)

The Wisdom in Scripture

Since wisdom is found in Christ, it is found also in his words. And the words of Scripture, as we have seen, are the words of Christ. Scripture is the word of God, who is the source of all wisdom. That means that Scripture should play a key role as a source for wisdom and knowledge.

The question of proper sources for knowledge and how to manage a search for knowledge is a key concern for human existence. Many people today want to conduct their search independently of God. They want to make up their own minds. They pay no attention to the Bible as God's word. But this is in deep tension with God's own purpose for mankind.[1] God intended that human beings should have fellowship with him that includes communication in language. We may illustrate this principle by many cases throughout the history of redemption.

When God created man, he made him "in the image of God" (Gen. 1:26–27). As an aspect of being the image, human beings have the capacity for personal fellowship with God. Genesis 1 records that God spoke to man right away concerning his role in creation: "And God blessed them. And God said to them, 'Be fruitful and multiply and fill the earth and subdue it'" (Gen. 1:28). God also gave a specific commandment: "And the LORD God commanded the man, saying, 'You may surely eat of every tree of the garden, but of the tree of the knowledge of good and evil you shall not eat, for in the day that you eat of it you shall surely die'" (Gen. 2:16–17).

God did not intend human beings to figure everything out merely by their own wits. He intended from the beginning that human beings should live in the environment of God's creation and learn things by observation (Gen. 2:19–20). But God's own words to mankind would have a central, directing role. God established fellowship with man, a person-to-person relationship.

---

[1] A similar point is found in Vern S. Poythress, foreword to *Apologetics: A Justification of Christian Belief*, by John M. Frame, 2nd ed. (Phillipsburg, NJ: P&R, 2015), xiii–xxviii.

This fellowship included the dimension of communication in language. God gave instructions through verbal communication. This communication, because it came from God himself, was to play a central, guiding role in human development.

When Adam and Eve rebelled against God, the rebellion took place in the context of satanic temptation. Satan endeavored to create confusion about whether they could trust the word of God: the Serpent said, "You will not surely die" (Gen. 3:4). Hearing and trusting the word of God becomes, if anything, *more* important subsequent to the fall, because human hearts are corrupted by the fall, and we ourselves desire to substitute our own words and thoughts for the word of God. Accordingly, the Scripture shows again and again how God calls his people to trust and obey his word, as a central source of guidance in their lives.

For example, God called Abram to leave Ur of the Chaldeans: "Now the LORD said to Abram, 'Go from your country and your kindred and your father's house to the land that I will show you. And I will make of you a great nation, and I will bless you and make your name great, so that you will be a blessing'" (Gen. 12:1–2). Abram had to trust that God's plan was better than his own, and he had to obey God's direction to go to the land of Canaan.

Later on, God called Abram to believe his word when it seemed impossible for him to have a son.

> And behold, the word of the LORD came to him: "This man shall not be your heir; your very own son shall be your heir." And he brought him outside and said, "Look toward heaven, and number the stars, if you are able to number them." Then he said to him, "So shall your offspring be." And he *believed* the LORD, and he counted it to him as righteousness. (Gen. 15:4–6)

God challenged Abram to believe that a son would come from Sarah, his wife: "Is anything too hard for the LORD? At the appointed time I will return to you, about this time next year, and

Sarah shall have a son" (Gen. 18:14). After Isaac was born, God called Abraham to sacrifice his son Isaac, placing the word of God above all his loves and hopes (Gen. 22:2).

Abraham's descendants multiplied and became the nation of Israel. God's speech continued to play a central role for Israel. He gave the Israelites the Ten Commandments as the fundamental basis for the nation (Ex. 19:5–6; 20:1–17).

God's word also had a central role during the conquest of the land of Canaan. At that time, God told Joshua to be diligent in keeping the law.

> Only be strong and very courageous, being careful to do according to *all the law* that Moses my servant commanded you. Do not turn from it to the right hand or to the left, that you may have good success wherever you go. *This Book of the Law* shall not depart from your mouth, but you shall meditate on it day and night, so that you may be careful to do according to all that is written in it. For then you will make your way prosperous, and then you will have good success. Have I not commanded you? Be strong and courageous. Do not be frightened, and do not be dismayed, for the LORD your God is with you wherever you go. (Josh. 1:7–9)

This pattern of centrality for God's words continues into the New Testament. For example, Jesus indicates the importance that his followers should attach to his words.

> Everyone then who hears *these words of mine* and does them will be like a wise man who built his house on the rock. And the rain fell, and the floods came, and the winds blew and beat on that house, but it did not fall, because it had been founded on the rock. And everyone who hears *these words of mine* and does not do them will be like a foolish man who built his house on the sand. And the rain fell, and the floods came, and the winds blew and beat against that house, and it fell, and great was the fall of it. (Matt. 7:24–27)

Wisdom comes not just from the words of Jesus, but also from *fellowship* with Jesus. We are supposed to build our lives on him and his words.

Other Sources of Knowledge

Scripture has a central role in human growth in knowledge, but it is not the *only* possible source of knowledge. God made the world, and he reveals himself in the world that he made (Ps. 19:1–6; Rom. 1:18–23). This revelation is called *general revelation*. God thereby gives knowledge even to unbelievers (1 Kings 4:31; Job 32:8–9; Ps. 94:10–11).

The book of Proverbs illustrates growth in this kind of knowledge. The book of Proverbs is a form of *special* revelation—it is the word of God to us. But it talks about the world around us and urges us to gain wisdom, partly through observing the world. That is, it affirms the positive role of *general* revelation. It focuses particularly on human life and what we can learn about wise and foolish behavior. Wisdom begins with "the fear of the LORD" (Prov. 1:7). We gain wisdom from listening to the wisdom of Proverbs. But Proverbs also invites us to observe keenly what goes on in the world.

So God indicates that we should learn from many sources outside the Bible. But we human beings are fallible, and our judgment is corrupted by the fall. General revelation through the world that God made is reliable, but our *interpretation* of it is subject to error. Thus, Scripture has a unique role as our infallible guide in knowledge.

Difference from the World

Followers of Christ are to keep his words. As we have already seen, that means that we should be intent on keeping all the words of Scripture, which is the word of God. We must not seek knowledge *autonomously*, in independence from or isolation from God's words. That is a form of rebellion, which dishonors God's way of living. When there seems to be a tension between God's word in Scripture and what we are learning from other sources, Scripture has the priority because it is the word of God.

In this respect, we who are followers of Christ live very differently from the rest of the world. We must beware of conforming to the world in the area of knowledge. Loyalty to Christ means loyalty to his words. This loyalty seems foolish to the world. But Christ is completely reliable. It is completely sensible to rely on him. It is completely foolish to reject his words and his guidance. What seems folly to the world is the wisdom of God: "Has not God made foolish the wisdom of the world? For since, in the wisdom of God, the world did not know God through wisdom, it pleased God through the *folly* of what we preach to save those who believe" (1 Cor. 1:20–21). As one aspect of following the wisdom of God, we receive his instruction faithfully and with trust.

Limitations in Understanding

That does not mean, however, that we overestimate our own *understanding* of Scripture. Though Scripture is infallible, our understanding of it is not. When there is a tension between what we think Scripture says and some other source, it is legitimate to revisit our *understanding* of Scripture. It is legitimate to inspect critically our own assumptions in reading and to ask whether Scripture is saying everything that we think it says. God can use this process to increase our knowledge.[2] It is also true that not everything in Scripture is equally clear. The central message of salvation is clear, but there are also mysteries. Scripture itself indicates that some things within it are difficult to interpret.

> Our beloved brother Paul also wrote to you according to the wisdom given him, as he does in all his letters when he speaks in them of these matters. There are some things in them that

---

[2] See Vern S. Poythress, *Redeeming Science: A God-Centered Approach* (Wheaton, IL: Crossway, 2006), chaps. 2–3.

are *hard to understand,* which the ignorant and unstable twist to their own destruction, as they do the other Scriptures. You therefore, beloved, knowing this beforehand, take care that you are not carried away with the error of lawless people and lose your own stability. But grow in the grace and knowledge of our Lord and Savior Jesus Christ. To him be the glory both now and to the day of eternity. Amen. (2 Pet. 3:15–18)

In our use of Scripture we need a proper sense of confidence and also of our limitations. We can be confident when Scripture speaks clearly; but we should be humble in acknowledging where we have limited knowledge.[3]

Christians of earlier generations understood both the clarity of Scripture and the need to acknowledge our limitations. The Westminster Confession of Faith summarizes well the interplay of confidence and limitations:

All things in Scripture are *not alike plain in themselves,* nor alike clear unto all: yet those things which are necessary to be known, believed, and observed for salvation are so *clearly propounded,* and opened in some place of Scripture or other, that not only the learned, but the unlearned, in a due use of the ordinary means, may attain unto a sufficient *understanding* of them.[4]

---

[3] I have tried to illustrate the process in Vern S. Poythress, *Inerrancy and the Gospels: A God-Centered Approach to the Challenges of Harmonization* (Wheaton, IL: Crossway, 2012); see also Poythress, *Inerrancy and Worldview: Answering Modern Challenges to the Bible* (Wheaton, IL: Crossway, 2012).
[4] Westminster Confession of Faith 1.7, italics mine.

5

Contrasts with the World

Our discussion up to this point has made clear that Christians who are serious about following Christ are different from the world. Just how different? Christians seek the instruction of Christ in Scripture and follow it. That is one of the basic differences. As a result, we differ from non-Christians all the way across the field of knowledge. Let us look briefly at some of the areas of difference.

Differences in Knowledge

Most obviously, we differ in our idea of what *standards* to use in sifting through claims to knowledge. Christians trust what God says in Scripture; non-Christians do not. We have already mentioned this difference in the previous chapter.

We also differ in *what* we know. Christians have a saving knowledge of God and of Christ that does not belong to the world.

> At that time Jesus declared, "I thank you, Father, Lord of heaven and earth, that you have hidden these things from the wise and understanding and *revealed them* to little children; yes, Father, for such was your gracious will." (Matt. 11:25–26)

O righteous Father, even though the world does not know you, I know you, and these *know* that you have sent me. I made *known* to them your name, and I will continue to make it *known*, that the love with which you have loved me may be in them, and I in them. (John 17:25–26)

For God, who said, "Let light shine out of darkness," has shone in our hearts to *give the light of the knowledge* of the glory of God in the face of Jesus Christ. (2 Cor. 4:6)

We also differ in how we *view* human knowledge. Christians know from Scripture that God is the original for all knowledge. By contrast, non-Christians want to imagine that their human knowledge has ultimate status. The difference between these views comes out dramatically with the fall of Adam and Eve. When Adam ate the forbidden fruit, he pretended that his own knowledge and judgments were better than God's.

What does it mean for God to be the original for all knowledge? God knows everything. We are made in the image of God, so we can have genuine knowledge. But it is derivative knowledge. Anything we know, we know because God knew it first. And knowledge is a *gift* from God. The fact that God is the source of knowledge is most obvious when we consider the knowledge of salvation, as mentioned above. But some verses indicate that God gives people all the knowledge they have—not merely saving knowledge:

But it is the spirit in man,
    the breath of the Almighty, that *makes him understand*.
      (Job 32:8)

He who disciplines the nations, does he not rebuke?
He who *teaches man knowledge*—
    the LORD—knows the thoughts of man,
    that they are but a breath. (Ps. 94:10–11)

Christian and non-Christians differ at this point. At least in principle, Christians acknowledge that their knowledge is derived from God and is subordinate to God's knowledge. Non-Christians do not.

Finally, Christians and non-Christians differ on the *context* in which they view their knowledge. Christians know not only that knowledge is from God but also that all truth is ordained by God. They acknowledge God as the source and fountain for truth. They praise God as they admire his goodness and wisdom and power displayed in the truths that they come to know. Non-Christians do not. Some may indeed praise a god that is a substitute for the true God—the god of Islam or one of the gods of the ancient Greek pantheon. Others may think of truth as impersonal—just out there. But they too depend on God without acknowledging him.[1]

In all these ways, Christians and non-Christians have opposing views. Their views are *antithetical* to each other. Cornelius Van Til terms this opposition the *antithesis* between Christian and non-Christian thought.[2] In other words, there are two ways of thinking, not one. These two ways spring from differences in basic commitments. Either your heart is inclined toward serving God or your heart is inclined to rebellion against him.

The Bible contains grim descriptions of the corruption of knowledge in the minds of unbelievers. Consider these words from the apostle Paul:

> Now this I say and testify in the Lord, that you must no longer walk as the Gentiles do, in the *futility* of their *minds*. They are darkened in their understanding, alienated from the life of God because of the ignorance that is in them, due to their hardness of heart. They have become callous and have given themselves up to sensuality, greedy to practice every kind of impurity. But that is not the way you learned Christ! (Eph. 4:17–20)

---

[1] Vern S. Poythress, *Redeeming Science: A God-Centered Approach* (Wheaton, IL: Crossway, 2006), chaps. 1 and 14.
[2] The word *antithesis* was also a key term for Abraham Kuyper, whom I will discuss later.

Compromises from Christians

But now we must also note that there are many compromises on both sides. Even genuine Christians, genuine followers of Christ, are not free from sin. The Holy Spirit radically transforms us when we are born again. But we need to continue to grow in holiness and in obedience to Christ. As long as we are on earth, we still have sinful tendencies in our minds and desires, and these break out in actual sins. The Bible teaches that every Christian sins: "If we say we have *no sin*, we deceive ourselves, and the truth is not in us. If we *confess our sins*, he is faithful and just to forgive us our sins and to cleanse us from all unrighteousness. If we say we have not sinned, we make him a liar, and his word is not in us" (1 John 1:8–10). These sins include sins in the *mind*. That is why the Bible says that you need to continue to be "transformed by the renewal of your mind" (Rom. 12:2).

Christians can fall into sin not only in subtle ways but also in obvious, grievous ways. The Bible contains notable examples of grievous sins committed by people who were saved. Peter denied the Lord three times (Matt. 26:30–34, 69–75). David committed adultery with Bathsheba and plotted to have her husband, Uriah, killed (2 Samuel 11). Peter and David were both forgiven later. These instances of forgiveness have a positive point. The grace of God provides forgiveness for gross sins as well as subtle sins. It is a shame when a Christian brings disgrace to the name of Christ by his sin. But it does happen. And the Bible talks about it frankly. Christians are not entirely consistent with the faith that they profess.

Inconsistencies from Non-Christians

In addition, non-Christians are not consistent in their unbelief and rebellion. What would it mean to be consistent in rebelling against God? It would mean rebelling against all his commandments and acting with complete selfishness and ruthlessness.

Sin goes deep. And if left to itself, it spreads like a cancer and corrupts people more and more. We can observe the downward spiral of sin especially in Genesis 6:1–7, where increasing corruption led to the judgment of the flood. As sin grows, people in their attempt to escape God may become more and more violently sinful. And they may become more sinful in their view of knowledge. For example, they may become skeptical about knowledge in general. Or they may lose knowledge because they refuse to accept it as a gift from God.

But God undertakes to restrain corruption. When people were cooperating with each other in proudly building the tower of Babel, God restrained the growth of wickedness by dividing their languages, which ended their cooperation. God restrains selfishness in many ways. People are not as bad as they could be. They may help others, though their motivations are still ultimately selfish—to maintain a good reputation by doing good, or to feel good about themselves because they have helped, or to win friends for themselves. Their actions look good outwardly, but they still fail to serve the glory of God.

Common Grace

In addition, we should observe that non-Christians receive many benefits from God. These benefits are often called *common grace*. In several passages the Bible indicates that God gives benefits to unbelievers.

God acts in kindness even toward his enemies: "For he makes his sun rise on the evil and on the good, and sends rain on the just and on the unjust" (Matt. 5:45). The apostle Paul makes a similar point in a sermon in Acts: "Yet he did not leave himself without witness, for he did *good* by giving you rains from heaven and fruitful seasons, satisfying your hearts with food and gladness" (Acts 14:17).

Likewise, Genesis 8:22 indicates that God gives everyone the benefits of a regular order in the world: "While the earth remains, seedtime and harvest, cold and heat, summer and winter, day and night, shall not cease." This passage is particularly significant. As a kind of foundation for common grace, it is sweeping in its scope. In terms of time, it spans "while the earth remains." It is also sweeping in the scope of its beneficiaries, because the subsequent passage, Genesis 9, includes all the descendants of Noah and all the animals as well.

Why does God give this promise to mankind? The verses preceding Genesis 8:22 explain:

> Then Noah built an altar to the LORD and took some of every clean animal and some of every clean bird and offered burnt offerings on the altar. And when the LORD smelled the pleasing aroma, the LORD said in his heart, "I will never again curse the ground because of man, for the intention of man's heart is evil from his youth. Neither will I ever again strike down every living creature as I have done. While the earth remains, seedtime and harvest, cold and heat, summer and winter, day and night, shall not cease." (Gen. 8:20–22)

Note that Noah offered animal sacrifices. These sacrifices were a "type" or shadow, pointing forward to the sacrifice of Christ. The animal sacrifices did not have value or power merely in themselves. God was pleased with them because they were connected to Christ. God's acceptance of them is vividly described in the words "when the LORD smelled the pleasing aroma" (v. 21). Sacrifices offered in faith formed the basis for God's kindness to Noah and his descendants.

We can see the same point by considering human guilt. People in rebellion against God do not deserve kindness. They deserve death (Rom. 6:23). Why do they get better than they deserve? They receive this kindness because of Christ. God is kind to human beings on the basis of the sacrifice of Christ.

We must avoid confusion here. The sacrifice of Christ has more than one benefit. Through his sacrifice, some people are saved eternally—but not everyone belongs to this category. *One of the* benefits is eternal salvation for those who are united to Christ. But through the symbolism of animal sacrifice, Genesis 8:20–22 indicates that there is another, minor benefit: even unbelievers get better than they deserve while they are in this life.

Common grace is distinct from the special, saving grace that comes to believers in Christ. It is *grace* because people do not deserve it. It comes as a benefit from Christ's work and his obedience. It is *common* because the benefits of seedtime and harvest are common to mankind; they are not confined to Christians.

The Bible talks in several places of physical benefits, such as God making the sun rise (Matt. 5:45) and "giving you rains from heaven and fruitful seasons, satisfying your hearts with food and gladness" (Acts 14:17). But the principle of common grace is a broad one. We can see that God gives *mental* benefits as well as physical benefits. He gives knowledge: "He who teaches man *knowledge*—the LORD . . ." (Ps. 94:10–11). That means that Christians may learn from non-Christians. Non-Christians may have many valuable insights. All of these insights are gifts from God. They are forms of common grace.

Antithesis and Common Grace

But we saw earlier that there is an *antithesis* between Christians and non-Christians. This antithesis affects how they think and how they act. So how is this antithesis consistent with common grace? It is consistent because the antithesis lies at the level of fundamental principles. It does not mean that either Christians or non-Christians act in ways fully consistent with the underlying fundamental principles they hold. Moreover, common grace mitigates the effects of the antithesis. Common grace acts partly to restrain the full expression of evil in the hearts of non-Christians.

So, depending on the circumstances, there can be many fruitful relationships between Christians and non-Christians. God enables fruitful interaction. For one thing, Christians and non-Christians live in the same world. God created the world and sustains it. God reveals himself through what he has made. As a result, non-Christians cannot escape God and his presence. Here is what Romans 1:18–23 says:

> For the wrath of God is revealed from heaven against all ungodliness and unrighteousness of men, who by their unrighteousness suppress the truth. For what can be known about God is plain to them, because God has shown it to them. For his invisible attributes, namely, his eternal power and divine nature, have been clearly perceived, ever since the creation of the world, in the things that have been made. So they are without excuse. For although they knew God, they did not honor him as God or give thanks to him, but they became futile in their thinking, and their foolish hearts were darkened. Claiming to be wise, they became fools, and exchanged the glory of the immortal God for images resembling mortal man and birds and animals and creeping things.

In addition, the presence of common grace means that Christians can learn from non-Christians. They can also cooperate in activities together, whether in work or in education or in art, when common grace allows it.

For example, a Christian and a non-Christian may work side by side as clerks in a supermarket. The Christian is serving Christ and looking for opportunities to bless the customers and bless the business and his fellow workers. The non-Christian may just be looking for the next paycheck. But at least he is honest. He is not stealing from the cash register and not repeatedly showing up late for work or taking unauthorized work breaks. His willingness to work is one effect of common grace. He may be willing to help the Christian, either because he is friendly and helpful by common grace or because he hopes to build a relationship that will enable him to ask for help when he needs it.

Limits to Cooperation

But there are limits to cooperation. Second Corinthians 6:14–16 indicates that Christian believers should not join in intimate partnerships with unbelievers:

> Do not be unequally *yoked* with unbelievers. For what *partnership* has righteousness with lawlessness? Or what *fellowship* has light with darkness? What accord has Christ with Belial? Or what portion does a believer share with an unbeliever? What agreement has the temple of God with idols? For we are the temple of the living God; as God said,
>
> > "I will make my dwelling among them and walk
> > among them,
> > and I will be their God,
> > and they shall be my people."

A Christian should not marry a non-Christian (1 Cor. 7:39). But the principle applies to other relationships as well. A Christian businessman wants his business to serve his employees with good wages and working conditions, and to serve the customers with good products, as well as to make some profit so that the business can keep going or even expand. Should he join in partnership with a non-Christian who thinks that the sole goal of business is to make money?

A Christian educator wants to found an educational institution that will open the minds of students to the wonders of God-given knowledge and encourage the praise of God. Should he join in partnership with a non-Christian who thinks that education should be based on the assumptions of materialist philosophy, that everything consists merely in matter and motion?

A Christian worker wants to join with fellow workers in negotiating working conditions that serve both the business and employees. Should he join in partnership with workers whose sole goal is to get as much as possible from management, with as little work as possible?

A simple answer cannot cover all situations. The principle of not being "unequally yoked" is a sound biblical principle, expressed in 2 Corinthians 6:14. But in just which settings does it directly apply? Conditions vary enormously. It takes wisdom to discern what kind of situation we are in, what kind of cooperation is being proposed, and what kind of consequences it may have. To some extent, this book is meant to be an introduction to how we may grow in wise living in these varied circumstances.

Such questions come up often in our lives. The questions become more excruciating when civil government is extending its power over business or education or labor or art. Civil government is supposed to exist for the benefit of all citizens, with all religious convictions. But when it compels people to work together at common goals, it can easily attempt to homogenize its citizens and suppress freedom in favor of bureaucratic uniformity. When it controls an educational institution, it suppresses minority expressions. In the United States, a Christian teacher in state-controlled elementary education cannot freely talk about God's relationship to what is being taught. Government-produced materials on sexually transmitted diseases cannot include advice that provides the religious basis for sexual purity.

Principles with Variations

We can be sure that the two fundamental principles of antithesis and common grace will continue to be at work while this age endures. Christian believers and unbelievers will continue to be radically different in their fundamental motivations and their views of the world. Their views are antithetical. At the same time, God's grace will continue to be at work, giving us space for various kinds of cooperation.

We cannot specify beforehand a system of rules that easily enables us to predict how antithesis and common grace work in particular circumstances. Antithesis will always be with us; but its expressions will vary over time as unbelievers shift from one form of idolatrous commitment to another, and shifts take place in various ways in particular fields of potential cooperation.

Common grace will also continue to be with us. But it cannot be taken for granted. It is, after all, *grace*. We do not deserve it, and we cannot claim it as our "right." Genesis 8:22 guarantees that there will be day and night, seedtime and harvest. But it does *not* guarantee that there will never be a shortage of food. It does not guarantee that there will never be destructive hurricanes. It does not guarantee that non-Christians in every culture and historical period will always be equally open to learning, or equally honest, or equally just, or equally tolerant of a Christian viewpoint. In fact, there may be times when intense persecution arises (Acts 14:22; 2 Tim. 3:12; Rev. 2:10). Christian living may sometimes take the form of life in prison, life radically out of harmony with other human beings who have power.

A Threefold Difference—in Person, Norm, and Situation

We can become more specific about ways in which believers and unbelievers differ from one another. First, they differ at the level of the heart. Believers have had their hearts renewed through the work of the Holy Spirit. They have been born again. Theologians call this change the work of *regeneration*.

Second, only believers recognize Christ as the Master and Lawgiver for our lives. And if Christ is the Lawgiver, Scripture is his "law." Believers receive Christ's instruction in Scripture with humility. Unbelievers differ concerning the norms for life.

Third, believers and unbelievers differ in their response to the presence of God in the world. God reveals his presence and his character.

> For what can be known about God is plain to them, because God has shown it to them. For his invisible attributes, namely, his eternal power and divine nature, have been *clearly perceived*, ever since the creation of the world, in the things that have been made. So they are without excuse. (Rom. 1:19–20)

The heavens *declare* the glory of God,
    and the sky above *proclaims* his handiwork.
Day to day pours out speech,
    and night to night reveals knowledge. (Ps. 19:1–2)

Believers recognize and acknowledge this revelation from God. Unbelievers suppress it (Rom. 1:18).

In sum, by regeneration, believers and unbelievers differ *existentially*, in their attitudes and their personal orientations. In adherence to norms, believers and unbelievers differ *normatively*. In response to universal revelation from God, believers and unbelievers differ *situationally*, in their understanding of the situation, the world in which they live. These three differences correspond respectively to John Frame's three perspectives on ethics: the existential perspective, the normative perspective, and the situational perspective.[3]

In Frame's discussion, the three perspectives interlock and lead to one another. Likewise, in the antithetical differences between believers and unbelievers, the three types of antithesis interlock. Each is in a sense an aspect of the other two. For example, unbelievers suppress the situational revelation of God in the world because they have unbelieving hearts (existential) and faulty norms (normative). They have faulty norms because they suppress God's revelation (situational) and have unbelieving hearts (existential).

---

[3] John M. Frame, *Perspectives on the Word of God: An Introduction to Christian Ethics* (Eugene, OR: Wipf & Stock, 1999); Frame, *The Doctrine of the Christian Life* (Phillipsburg, NJ: P&R, 2008).

Part 2

RESOURCES FOR
SERVING CHRIST

6

Basic Spiritual Resources

The Bible indicates that God provides basic spiritual resources that instruct and empower us to serve Christ. What are they? Many Christians already know of those fundamental resources. But in this chapter we briefly review them, as a reminder to those familiar with them and as an incentive for those who are just now getting started.

The Power of the Resurrection

The first resource is the power of Christ's resurrection. Christ was raised to life on the third day (1 Cor. 15:4). His resurrection is the resurrection of one who *represents* us, just as Adam represented humanity when he fell into sin (Rom. 5:12–21). Christ's rising from the grave results in resurrection life coming to those who believe in him.

> We were buried therefore with him by baptism into death, in order that, just as Christ was raised from the dead by the glory of the Father, we too might *walk in newness of life*. (Rom. 6:4)

> If then *you have been raised with Christ*, seek the things that are above, where Christ is, seated at the right hand of God. Set

your minds on things that are above, not on things that are on earth. For you have died, and your life is hidden with Christ in God. (Col. 3:1–3)

Since Christ was raised, and since we who believe in him are united to him, Christ's power is at work in us: "If the Spirit of him who raised Jesus from the dead dwells in you, he who raised Christ Jesus from the dead will also *give life* to your mortal bodies through his Spirit who dwells in you" (Rom. 8:11).

The Holy Spirit

The second resource is the Holy Spirit. Christ sends the Holy Spirit to dwell in us. By the Spirit we walk in the way of holiness, as the following passages illustrate:

> You, however, are not in the flesh but *in the Spirit*, if in fact the Spirit of God dwells in you. Anyone who does not have the Spirit of Christ does not belong to him. But if Christ is in you, although the body is dead because of sin, the Spirit is life because of righteousness. (Rom. 8:9–10)

> But *the fruit of the Spirit* is love, joy, peace, patience, kindness, goodness, faithfulness, gentleness, self-control; against such things there is no law. And those who belong to Christ Jesus have crucified the flesh with its passions and desires. If we live by the Spirit, let us also keep in step with the Spirit. (Gal. 5:22–25)

The Holy Spirit is essential if we are to obey Christ as he deserves, and if we are to make any progress at all in Christian living. We cannot do it ourselves. God must work in us: "Work out your own salvation with fear and trembling, for it is God who *works in you*, both to will and to work for his good pleasure" (Phil. 2:12–13).

The presence of the Holy Spirit and the resurrection power of Christ means that Christians lead renewed lives. But, as we have said before, they are not sinless. When they sin, the Bible says that they should confess their sins. Through Christ they receive forgiveness (1 John 1:9).

The Means of Grace

The next resource is "the means of grace." As mentioned earlier, the means of grace include Bible reading, Bible study, listening to preaching, prayer, singing praises to God, participating in the sacraments (baptism and the Lord's Supper), and fellowship with God's people. In all this, the church is important.

America is a country overrun by individualism. And this attitude of individualism unfortunately flows over into the practice of Christian living. Christians often do not realize the importance of the church. God designed us so that we would grow spiritually not merely by private time with the Bible and with prayer. God gave us his church. The church is called "the body of Christ," and each member has a contribution to make to the functioning of the whole body (1 Cor. 12:12–31).

The church is not perfect in this age. It is filled with people like us, who are contaminated by sin but have come to seek God's grace. But God intends us to participate in the church, not just to live as isolated believers. Unbelievers also are welcome to come to church meetings in search of God. But membership in the church is for God's family, those who belong to God by faith in Christ.[1]

---

[1] I grew up a Baptist, but I have come to the conviction that the church should baptize the infant children of believers; these children also belong to the community. See Vern S. Poythress, "Indifferentism and Rigorism in the Church: With Implications for Baptizing Small Children," *Westminster Theological Journal* 59, no. 1 (1997): 13–29, , accessed July 9, 2014, http://www.frame-poythress .org/indifferentism-and-rigorism/; Poythress, "Linking Small Children with Infants in the Theology of Baptizing," *Westminster Theological Journal* 59, no. 2 (1997): 143–58, accessed July 9, 2014, http://www.frame-poythress.org/linking-small-children-with-infants-in-the-theology-of-baptizing/. It would deflect from the main focus to take up the question of children at this point.

7

Resources from Theology,
Especially the Reformation

Theological writings of generations both past and present offer an important resource when we are considering the transformation of the mind. The best theology aids us in transforming our minds. Theology is a summary of the Bible's teaching on various subjects. We learn theology from the Bible itself, of course. And the Bible is the only infallible written source for such teaching. We ought to use the Bible as we sift through good and bad ideas in human writings.

But human writings in theology are still a valuable resource because God has created us to work in communities. We learn from others. The body of Christ has many members making up one body (Rom. 12:4–5; 1 Cor. 12:12–14). Those who write theology are among those members. And the writings in theology come not only from the present time but also from the past, so that we can profit from the insights of generations and generations of the best reflections on Scripture.

The Heritage of the Reformation: Principles of Salvation

I have profited the most from the *Reformed* tradition in theology. Because this tradition sees the Bible as the only infallible verbal source for theology, it endeavors to submit thoroughly to the Bible's teaching, as it should. That is fundamental. In addition, it is characterized by other theological convictions, based on the Bible. These include the principle of the sovereign rule of God over all things and the sovereign power of God in salvation. The conviction about God's sovereignty had an important role in the teaching of Saint Augustine and subsequently influenced the entire Western church. It is obviously pertinent to the principle of the lordship of Christ.

In addition, the Reformed tradition includes the basic principles rediscovered at the time of the Reformation:

- the principle that we should use Scripture alone—not church traditions—as the only infallible source for doctrine;
- the principle that salvation is by God's grace alone, not by human merit, and not by a *combination* of grace and merit;
- the principle that salvation comes through faith alone, faith in Christ—we are not justified by faith *plus* works;
- the principle that salvation displays solely the glory of God, with no human boasting;
- the principle that salvation is found in Christ alone. Salvation does not come partly from human mediators like priests, nor partly from self-appointed paths to direct union with God (mysticism).

These principles are often summarized in Latin as *sola scriptura* (by Scripture alone), *sola gratia* (by grace alone), *sola fide* (by faith alone), *soli deo gloria* (to the glory of God alone), and *solus Christus* (Christ alone). The principles belong not only to the Reformed tradition but also to the Lutheran tradition (Martin Luther held to all of them). And some Anabaptists would have felt a kinship with some of them. Modern Bible-believing Baptists and Wesleyans would also hold to some of them.

The Priesthood of All Believers

In addition to these basic principles about the nature of salvation, the Reformation saw the development of two key concepts that encouraged the acknowledgment of Christ as Lord of all. First, the principal Reformers emphasized the *priesthood of all believers*. This is closely related to the principle of Christ alone (*solus Christus*). It includes the idea that Christ alone is our all-sufficient High Priest. He has reconciled us to God by atoning for our sins in his own body and by presenting himself as our High Priest before the Father, to intercede on our behalf: "Consequently, he [Christ] is able to save to the uttermost those who draw near to God through him, since he always lives to *make intercession for them*" (Heb. 7:25).

Christ has brought to fulfillment all the symbolism in the Old Testament priesthood. Consequently, believers are free through Christ to approach God (Heb. 10:19–22). They do not need the intervention of other human intermediaries, such as the Roman Catholic priests or the dead saints (Mary, Peter, John, etc.).

The principle of the priesthood of believers has implications for believers' relationship to the Bible. Through Christ, the Holy Spirit comes as a gift to all believers and teaches them as they read Scripture. So ordinary believers, not only the clergy, should have access to God's Word and study it. This principle has led to the translation of the Bible into the languages of the people.

The priesthood of believers provides resources for actually carrying into practice the lordship of Christ over all of life. As believers read the Bible, they receive encouragement and empowering and principles to guide them in serving Christ in their lives. Christ's commands and instructions come to them with force and clarity because they have access to the very Word of God.

The Idea of Vocation

The Reformation also set forth the idea of *vocation* in a new way. In modern English, the word *vocation* most often describes a person's main line of work. Merriam-Webster's dictionary includes the following definition: "the work in which a person is employed: occupation."[1]

That definition is in line with a key idea of the Reformation, namely, that God has called (Latin *voco*) each believer to serve the Lord through his work. All biblically lawful forms of work are honorable when done to serve Christ and to promote his glory. The candle maker can please God just as much as the minister in the pulpit. This Reformational view contrasts sharply with the medieval Roman Catholic view, which distinguished "religious" vocations as holy and superior. In medieval times people entered the priesthood or became monks or nuns because they thought that only this kind of life could really be holy.

The Reformational idea of vocation makes an important contribution to understanding the real significance of the universal lordship of Christ. Jesus is Lord of all aspects of life, not just a narrowly "religious" life lived in a cloister. Christ is Lord of the candle maker and his candle making, of the merchant and his trade, of the schoolmaster and his teaching; he is not merely the Lord over the routines of prayer, song, and Bible reading in a monastery.

So a father and mother are serving the Lord if they work faithfully to raise their children. A person who works at a customer help desk or at a checkout counter may serve him as well.

The Reformed Tradition

From the Reformation developed several sub-traditions—Lutheran, Reformed, and Anabaptist (Mennonite). The Anglicans can also be considered an English subdivision of the Reformed

---

[1] "Vocation," in *Free Merriam-Webster Dictionary*, online, sense 2.a, accessed July 16, 2014, http://www.merriam-webster.com/dictionary/vocation.

tradition. Later came the Baptists and the Methodists. Sometimes the Reformed tradition is called *Calvinism*, after John Calvin.[2] A major Reformer at Geneva, Switzerland, Calvin synthesized the insights from Reformers before him, including Martin Luther, Ulrich Zwingli, Johannes Oecolampadius, and Martin Bucer. He also learned from earlier generations, especially Saint Augustine. The Reformers respected the writings of the Fathers from the ancient church, but they treated these writings as subordinate to Scripture. In the generations after Calvin, others built on the Reformed tradition.

The Reformed tradition is valuable when we consider the transformation of the mind and questions about the relationship of the Christian faith to the surrounding society and culture. Over the centuries, the Reformed tradition has devoted much attention to these questions, and even some people outside the tradition recognize that it has displayed strength and depth in biblically based treatment of the issues of the mind and of culture.

Why so? Partly because the Reformed tradition emphasizes the sovereignty of God as taught in Scripture. This principle of sovereignty includes the insight that Christ is Lord over all of life. Another reason is that the Reformed tradition emphasizes the radical corruption of mankind through the entrance of sin. Sin corrupts the mind as well as the desires of the body. It corrupts knowledge (Eph. 4:17–20). So we must take with great seriousness the obligation to "be transformed by the renewal of your mind" (Rom. 12:2). Renewal begins with regeneration by the Holy Spirit, who transforms a person's heart. It continues as the Holy Spirit sanctifies a person by the means of grace.

The Fallibility of Human Theology

We should also say that no theological tradition is perfect. Sins and erroneous paths crop up within any historical tradition. The

---

[2] His most famous work is *Institutes of the Christian Religion* (many editions), a summary of systematic theology.

Reformed tradition officially recognizes this reality in one of its central confessional documents, the Westminster Confession of Faith: "All synods or councils, since the Apostles' times, whether general or particular, may *err*; and many have *erred*. Therefore they are not to be made the rule of faith, or practice; but to be used as a help in both" (31.4, italics mine). According to this account, the Reformed tradition is "to be used as a help" in matters of faith and practice. But all tradition must be inspected critically on the basis of Scripture (WCF 2.1). That is why the Westminster Confession indicates that the confession itself is fallible, while Scripture is infallible, completely without error.

8

Abraham Kuyper and
His Successors

Now we turn to consider Abraham Kuyper (1837–1920) and his contributions. We had occasion earlier to reflect on a famous quote from Kuyper: "No single piece of our mental world is to be hermetically sealed off from the rest, and there is not a square inch in the whole domain of our human existence over which Christ, who is Sovereign over *all*, does not cry: 'Mine!'"[1] Kuyper is a key figure in discussions of Christ's lordship over all of life because he encouraged thoughtful obedience on the part of Christ's followers. It is worthwhile for us to look briefly at his life and legacy.[2]

---

[1] Abraham Kuyper, "Sphere Sovereignty," in *Abraham Kuyper: A Centennial Reader*, ed. James D. Bratt (Grand Rapids, MI: Eerdmans, 1998), 488, italics original. The quote was originally part of Kuyper's speech at the inauguration of the Free University of Amsterdam in 1880.

[2] James D. Bratt, *Abraham Kuyper: Modern Calvinist, Christian Democrat* (Grand Rapids, MI: Eerdmans, 2013), offers a full biography. Smaller contributions can be found in Jan de Bruijn, *Abraham Kuyper: A Pictorial Biography* (Grand Rapids, MI: Eerdmans, 2014); James Edward McGoldrick, *God's Renaissance Man: The Life and Work of Abraham Kuyper* (Darlington, UK: Evangelical Press, 2000); Richard J. Mouw, *Abraham Kuyper: A Short and Personal Introduction* (Grand Rapids, MI: Eerdmans, 2011). Biographical summaries can be found in Abraham Kuyper, *Lectures on Calvinism: Six Lectures Delivered at Princeton University under Auspices of the L. P. Stone Foundation* (Grand Rapids, MI: Eerdmans, 1931), i–vii; Bratt, *Abraham Kuyper: A Centennial Reader*, 4–16.

The Life of Kuyper

Abraham Kuyper's father was a minister in the Dutch Reformed Church in the Netherlands. Abraham himself attended Leiden University and was infected with liberal theology there. In 1863, while in graduate school, he experienced a conversion and later that year became a minister in the Dutch Reformed Church in the town of Beesd. A few years later, he fully embraced orthodox Reformed theology.

Kuyper became a key leader in a movement to work out in practice the implications of Christ's lordship in various areas of society. He was influenced by the political and theological ideas of Guillaume Groen van Prinsterer (1801–1876). Groen and Kuyper became leaders in the Reformed political party known as the Anti-Revolutionary Party. This party resisted the cultural influence of the Enlightenment and the French Revolution in the direction of atheism. Groen van Prinsterer was already exploring the implications of Christ's lordship in the political sphere. Kuyper expanded the vision to encompass other areas of life.

The Teachings of Kuyper

One of Kuyper's key ideas was "sphere sovereignty." He argued that God had appointed distinct social spheres with distinct responsibilities. Family, state, and church should be clearly distinguished. Each kind of social organization had "sovereignty" in a particular sphere. It should not encroach on the responsibilities of other spheres. This theory had the effect of limiting state power to the responsibilities of enforcing justice and equity. It contrasted with the idea, coming from the French Revolution, that the state had universal sovereignty over all of life.

Kuyper wrote a prodigious amount, including academic works on theology (e.g., *Principles of Sacred Theology*),[3] devotional pieces, and practical political articles. I have mentioned his active

---

[3] Abraham Kuyper, *Principles of Sacred Theology*, trans. J. Hendrik de Vries (Grand Rapids, MI: Eerdmans, 1968).

participation in politics as part of the Anti-Revolutionary Party. He then became prime minister of the Netherlands and advocated a policy whereby the government would not, by means of taxation and subsidies, favor any particular organizations just because they were founded on religious or antireligious principles. In 1880 Abraham Kuyper founded the Free University of Amsterdam, which was designed to operate according to Reformed religious principles.

After Kuyper's embrace of Reformed orthodoxy, he worked consistently to promote the lordship of Christ. His vision concerning the implications of lordship came to vigorous expression in his book *Lectures on Calvinism*, based on six lectures originally given at Princeton Seminary in 1898.[4] The lectures form the main chapters of the book: (1) "Calvinism a Life-system," (2) "Calvinism and Religion," (3) "Calvinism and Politics," (4) "Calvinism and Science," (5) "Calvinism and Art," and (6) "Calvinism and the Future." By means of these topics, Kuyper affirmed the lordship of Christ over all areas of life. And he maintained that Christ's lordship actually makes a practical difference for thought and action in every area, including politics, science, and art. Similar ideas are also found in his lecture given at the inauguration of the Free University of Amsterdam in 1880.[5] From this lecture comes the famous declaration of Christ's lordship over every "square inch in the whole domain of our human existence."[6]

The Neo-Kuyperian Movement

Kuyper's ideas have continued to have influence in the twentieth and twenty-first centuries, especially among Reformed thinkers and activists in the Netherlands, the United States, and Canada. His concepts have especially influenced a group of thinkers sometimes

---

[4] See also Peter S. Heslam, *Creating a Christian Worldview: Abraham Kuyper's Lectures on Calvinism* (Grand Rapids, MI: Eerdmans, 1998). The subtitle of Kuyper's *Lectures on Calvinism* incorrectly places the lectures at Princeton University instead of the seminary, but see p. ii in that work.
[5] Abraham Kuyper, "Sphere Sovereignty," in Bratt, *Abraham Kuyper: A Centennial Reader*, 461–90.
[6] Ibid., 488.

called "neo-Kuyperians," among whom Herman Dooyeweerd (1894–1977) was the most prominent.[7] Dooyeweerd endeavored to develop a distinctively Christian philosophy, called *cosmonomic* philosophy. In addition to Dooyeweerd there were D. H. Th. Vollenhoven (1892–1978), J. P. A. Mekkes (1898–1987), Hendrik G. Stoker (1899–1993), K. J. Popma (1903–1986), S. U. Zuidema (1906–1975), Hendrik van Riessen (1911–2000), H. Evan Runner (1916–2002), Robert D. Knudsen (1924–2000), and others. Within a larger circle of influence we may include also Hans R. Rookmaaker and Francis A. Schaeffer.[8] Cornelius Van Til (1895–1987) was sympathetic with this circle in its early stages but later became critical of Dooyeweerd's ideas.[9]

The neo-Kuyperians influenced by Dooyeweerd and his associates may be distinguished from the wider group of Kuyperians, those who have embraced Kuyper's principle that Christ is Lord of all of life. That is, the neo-Kuyperians are a subgroup. To this day we find, on the one hand, people who are heavily influenced by Dooyeweerd and cosmonomic philosophy (neo-Kuyperians) and, on the other hand, people who embrace the Kuyperian principle in a broad sense but either are not familiar with cosmonomic philosophy or have disagreements with it.

In addition, among the broad circle of Kuyperians, people may follow Abraham Kuyper's ideas more closely or more distantly.

---

[7] A good introduction can be found in L. Kalsbeek, *Contours of a Christian Philosophy: An Introduction to Herman Dooyeweerd's Thought*, ed. Bernard and Josina Zylstra (Toronto: Wedge, 1975). A historical introduction to Dooyeweerd and the larger movement is provided by Bernard Zylstra in ibid., 14–33. For critical assessment, see William D. Dennison, "Dutch Neo-Calvinism and the Roots of Transformation," *Journal of the Evangelical Theological Society* 42, no. 2 (1999): 271–91; John M. Frame, *A History of Western Philosophy and Theology* (Phillipsburg, NJ: P&R, 2015), 517–21; John M. Frame and Leonard Coppes, *The Amsterdam Philosophy: A Preliminary Critique* (Phillipsburg, NJ: Harmony, 1972); Vern S. Poythress, *Redeeming Philosophy: A God-Centered Approach to the Big Questions* (Wheaton, IL: Crossway, 2014), appendix A.

[8] H. R. Rookmaaker, *The Complete Works of Hans R. Rookmaaker* (Carlisle, PA: Piquant, 2003); Linette Martin, *Hans Rookmaaker: A Biography* (Downers Grove, IL: InterVarsity Press, 1979); Francis A. Schaeffer, *The Complete Works of Francis A. Schaeffer: A Christian Worldview* (Wheaton, IL: Crossway, 1985).

[9] Cornelius Van Til, "Response by C. Van Til" to Herman Dooyeweerd, in *Jerusalem and Athens: Critical Discussions on the Theology and Apologetics of Cornelius Van Til*, ed. E. R. Geehan (Nutley, NJ: Presbyterian and Reformed, 1971), 89–127. My colleague John Frame and I, both influenced by Van Til, have been appreciative of some aspects of cosmonomic philosophy, but also critical. We have accordingly gone our own way (see Frame and Coppes, *The Amsterdam Philosophy*; Poythress, *Redeeming Philosophy*, appendix A).

Some followers may try to build positively on nearly everything that Kuyper did. Others accept the general principle of Christ's universal lordship and admire Kuyper for his devotion to the cause, but may be critical of some of the details in the way that Kuyper himself worked out the implications of this principle. For example, there are disagreements over Kuyper's idea of common grace. Does common grace create some spaces where believers and unbelievers may work without serious differences? Or is the more fundamental influence the direction of one's heart, which generates differences everywhere else?[10] And in what ways might Scripture address particular intellectual issues as well as the direction of the heart?

Value from the Kuyperian Legacy

There is much of value in the legacy from Kuyper himself and from the Kuyperians. For a century or more, Kuyper's vision and his energy have empowered a larger movement. Kuyper and his successors have produced an impressive body of ideas and literature, and they have encouraged influential individuals and organizations that produced real change in the culture of the Netherlands. We can learn from their ideas and their attempts to influence society. We can receive inspiration from their zeal for the lordship of Christ. In our own lives, we can never be too zealous for loving Christ and serving him. We should never give up looking for new ways to serve, and new ways of purifying and intensifying our service.

But, in hindsight, we may also have questions about what happened in the long run. As I write, we are approaching the hundredth year after Kuyper's death, and the hundred-and-fortieth year after he founded the Free University of Amsterdam. Kuyper's

---

[10] Note the serious word of caution and criticism of Kuyper due to ambiguities in his idea of common grace: Branson Parler, "Two Cities or Two Kingdoms? The Importance of the Ultimate in Reformed Social Thought," in *Kingdoms Apart: Engaging the Two Kingdoms Perspective*, ed. Ryan C. McIlhenny (Phillipsburg, NJ: P&R, 2012), 173–97, esp. 180; William D. Dennison, "Van Til and Common Grace," *Mid-America Journal of Theology* 9 (1993): 225–47. See also Klaas Schilder, *Christ and Culture*, trans. G. van Rongen and W. Helder (Winnipeg: Premier, 1977), accessed February 6, 2015, http://www.reformed.org/webfiles/cc/christ_and_culture.pdf; and D. A. Carson, *Christ and Culture Revisited* (Grand Rapids, MI: Eerdmans, 2008), 212–16.

ideas are still motivating people to serve Christ with all their heart and to acknowledge Jesus as the Lord of all of life. But forces of secularization and liberal theology have taken a toll in the Netherlands. Orthodox faith and orthodox theology still exist there, but they belong to a remnant.

What happened? The history of Kuyper's influence in the United States, Canada, and other countries is complicated. Wherever we look, it is hard to avoid admitting that the luster and excitement that belonged to earlier generations of Kuyperians has somewhat faded. We may draw at least two conclusions. First, serving Christ the Lord in all of life is not as easy as it might appear. Sin can all too easily creep in stealthily and corrupt our work. Second, however fervently we serve him, we cannot guarantee earth-shattering results.

> Unless the LORD builds the house,
>   those who build it labor in vain.
> Unless the LORD watches over the city,
>   the watchman stay awake in vain. (Ps. 127:1)

If we look only at the past or at the present state of things, we might well become discouraged about Kuyper's program. Has it failed to leave a lasting legacy? In response, let us remember the essential point: Christ has "all authority in heaven and on earth" (Matt. 28:18). He is ruling. And our calling is to serve him with all our heart and soul and mind (Matt. 22:37). We are to serve him every hour of every day, in every sphere of life.

> And whatever you do, in word or deed, *do everything* in the name of the Lord Jesus, giving thanks to God the Father through him. (Col. 3:17)

> *Whatever you do*, work heartily, as *for the Lord* and not for men, knowing that from the Lord you will receive the inheritance as your reward. You are *serving the Lord Christ*. (Col. 3:23–24)

The reward comes from Christ. In the end, it does not matter whether we achieve little or much in the eyes of the world. What matters is his approval. We want to hear him say, "Well done, good and faithful servant" (Matt. 25:21, 23).

So, if we must, let us start again from the beginning in the process of learning to honor Christ as Lord and learning to encourage others also. We have the same Holy Spirit whom Christ poured out on the day of Pentecost (Acts 2:33). We have the Scriptures, the word of God, that he has provided for our instruction and nourishment. And, subordinate to these, we have now the additional writings, fallible though they be, of past generations of Kuyperians, as well as *critics* of the Kuyperians, from whom we may also learn.

9

Newer Resources

In addition to contributions by Abraham Kuyper himself and his neo-Kuyperian successors of the first generation, other resources are valuable in advancing his vision of serving Christ as the Lord of life.

Biblical Theology

Our first resource is biblical theology in the tradition of Geerhardus Vos (1862–1949).[1] The term *biblical theology* means quite a few things to different people.[2] It does not mean merely "a theology that is based on the Bible." That should be true of all sound theology. Rather, biblical theology studies the Bible with a focus on the *history* of revelation, going from creation and Adam forward to the consummation. It is also possible, within this expansive approach, to devote attention to the distinctive features of one part of the Bible or one human author. So we may speak of "Pauline theology" or "Johannine theology." We may also consider particular themes that run through the Bible, like the theme of offspring or the theme

---

[1] Geerhardus Vos, *Biblical Theology: Old and New Testaments* (Carlisle, PA: Banner of Truth, 1975).
[2] Vern S. Poythress, "Kinds of Biblical Theology," *Westminster Theological Journal* 70, no. 1 (2008): 129–42.

of the temple or the theme of covenants. All these ways of studying the Bible should be conducted with the guiding conviction that the Bible is divine revelation, not merely human reflection.

Well-done biblical theology has proved itself valuable in deepening our understanding of the Bible, contributing to healthier systematic theology, and encouraging robust preaching.[3] In these ways it contributes to enhancing the spiritual health of the church. And by contributing to the health of the church it serves God and Christ the Lord. So indirectly it contributes to the Kuyperian vision of acknowledging Christ as Lord in all of life.

But *many* useful things might be said to contribute to the health of the church. Is there some other way in which biblical theology may help?

Biblical theology as the story of creation, fall, and redemption provides us with a robust framework for understanding the complexities of life in a fallen world (see chap. 2, "The Story of Redemption," above).[4] In line with the affirmation that God created the world and rules over it, we affirm the goodness of what God created (1 Tim. 4:4–5). In line with the biblical teaching about the radical rebellion of mankind in the fall (Genesis 3; Rom. 5:12–21), we take seriously the massive corruption of the world and the cultures of the world. In line with the New Testament affirmations of the comprehensive character of Christ's work of salvation (Col. 1:20), we understand that redemption has effects on every aspect of life. In line with the biblical hope for the consummation of all things in the new heaven and the new earth (Rev. 21:1–22:5), we understand that the present forms of society do not last forever.

Applying Biblical Theology to Science

I have already mentioned biblical theology's usefulness in exploring various themes and how they develop and unfold in the history

---

[3] Richard B. Gaffin, Jr., "Systematic Theology and Biblical Theology," *Westminster Theological Journal* 38, no. 3 (1976): 281–99.
[4] See also the helpful contribution by D. A. Carson, *Christ and Culture Revisited* (Grand Rapids, MI: Eerdmans, 2008), esp. 44–65.

of redemption. Exploring these themes contributes directly to the program of acknowledging Christ as Lord of the mind in every academic sphere.

Take as an example the study of various natural sciences. Biblical theology can throw light on discussions in this field. Is Christ Lord of science? He is. But what difference does his lordship make here? Is science a religiously neutral discipline? Kuyper said no, and I agree.[5] But many people still think of science as neutral. If it were neutral, would the lordship of Christ make a Christian scientist different only in the sense of being more moral, more diligent, more honest, and more kind to his colleagues? It certainly ought to make a difference in all these ways. But does it make a difference in our very understanding of science as well? Does God call on Christians to think differently about science?

One main difficulty here is that God caused the Bible to be written before the rise of modern science. We can see in a general way that some parts of the Bible are relevant to science. For example, God's instruction in Genesis 1:28–30 for man to exercise dominion could be an encouragement for science. But the Bible does not provide us with an extended discussion that is devoted directly to the topic of modern science. The lack of discussion is one reason why people are tempted to think of science as religiously neutral.

As science grew in cultural importance over the past few centuries, theologians naturally saw the importance of discussing its meaning from a theological point of view. They also had to deal with apparent tensions between the Bible and science, which arose as scientists began to claim that the universe is a mechanism, that it is old, and that life has gradually evolved by unguided forces (Darwinism). It seemed that the primary way for theologians to

---

[5] Abraham Kuyper, "Calvinism and Science,"chap. 4 in *Lectures on Calvinism: Six Lectures Delivered at Princeton University under Auspices of the L. P. Stone Foundation* (Grand Rapids, MI: Eerdmans, 1931), 110–41 (note, however, that Kuyper was using the word *science* in a broad way, close to the idea of "academic disciplines"); Vern S. Poythress, *Redeeming Science: A God-Centered Approach* (Wheaton, IL: Crossway, 2006).

enter the discussion would have to be by using the resources of existing systematic theology, combined with a certain amount of philosophical reflection, in order to build a bridge between theology and science. For the most part, this is how major theologians like Abraham Kuyper, Herman Bavinck, and Cornelius Van Til interacted with science.

UNDERSTANDING SCIENTIFIC LAW AS GOD'S SPEECH

But biblical theology offers us other resources, because we can learn to ask a new set of questions as we study the Bible. It turns out that the Bible is more directly relevant to science than earlier generations may have realized. One theme to explore in biblical theology is the theme of God's word—God's speech. The Bible is the word of God. But the Bible also contains quite a few references to God governing the world by speaking and issuing commands:

> And God *said*, "Let there be light," and there was light.
> (Gen. 1:3)

> By the *word* of the LORD the heavens were made,
> and by the *breath* of his mouth all their host. (Ps. 33:6)

> He upholds the universe by the *word* of his power.
> (Heb. 1:3)

The real "law" governing the universe is God's speech. When scientists undertake to study the laws of the universe, they are actually studying God's speech. So science turns out to have a much more direct relation to scriptural teaching about God's speech than most people would have imagined. Moreover, what a scientist thinks about God (or a God substitute) influences what he thinks about scientific laws.

If God is personal, then his speech is his personal word. Because he is a faithful God, his speech will display his faithfulness. So there will be consistency in how he governs the world. We can depend on regularities such as the regular succession of day and night. We can also depend on the regularities of a less obvious kind, the regularities represented by the laws that scientists discover. On the other hand, because God is personal, there may be surprises. He may have reasons for doing something out of the ordinary for the sake of blessing his people. These exceptions are called miracles.

Now consider what happens when scientists no longer believe in the personal God of the Bible. They still believe in scientific laws. They have to, or they would stop being scientists. But they regard the laws as *impersonal*, more like a mechanism. And if laws are a mechanism, there can be no exceptions. Such scientists believe that miracles are impossible. And for God to come in Christ to create a new heaven and a new earth seems to them impossible.

Thus, Christians who pay attention to the Bible have a different conception of scientific law than does a non-Christian scientist who believes in impersonal law.

We have arrived at this insight beginning with the biblical teaching about God's speech, his word governing the universe. This particular use of biblical theology is only the beginning. A number of other biblical themes throw light on how we think about science; they even have relevance to the conception of particular sciences, like biology, chemistry, and physics.[6]

Biblical theology as conceived by Geerhardus Vos grew up during the twentieth century. Only gradually did systematic theologians learn how to appropriate it for their own task. So, from the standpoint of the Kuyperian theme of Christ as Lord, biblical theology is a comparatively new resource. And it is an important one whose potential has barely begun to be tapped.

REINING IN BOTH PHILOSOPHY AND SIMPLISTIC ANSWERS

Biblical theology becomes even more important because it helps to protect us from moving too far away from the specifics in the

---

[6] Poythress, *Redeeming Science*.

Bible as we interact with modern life. Science is not the only area in modern life that seems to be remote from cultures mentioned in the Bible. Because the cultures differ throughout time, we are easily tempted to think that the Bible itself is remote and has little to say to many areas in modern life.

Two enticing paths. So how do we come to appreciate what the Bible has to say specifically about science? The Bible *does* have implications for science. But how do we see these implications? We may be tempted in two directions. In one direction lies a secularist approach to science. This direction says that science has nothing to do with theology, and it can therefore safely be conducted in a religiously neutral way, with no attention to God or his Word. This is the direction that Kuyper vigorously repudiated (and rightly so). If Christ is Lord of all, he is Lord of science and Lord of business and Lord of media and Lord of entertainment and Lord of sports.

In the other direction lies a subtler problem. If we want to bring our Christian faith into relation to these new areas characterizing the modern world, we do it almost wholly through philosophy. We try to build a general system of Christian philosophy, and through this general system we have a framework whose principles are general enough so that we can apply them to modern life.

All this is good, provided our philosophy is sound. But it has proved notoriously difficult for Christians to produce sound philosophy. Most of Western philosophy has been the history of trying to answer the major questions of life independently of divine revelation, by reason alone. And that policy of ignoring divine revelation is a recipe for autonomy in human thinking rather than submission to God's instruction. Christians over the centuries have tried their hand at reforming philosophy. But it has mostly taken the form of reforms that were not radical enough, reforms that still did not root out the underlying principle of autonomy.[7]

Even when Christians are thinking about modern questions—in

---

[7] John M. Frame, *A History of Western Philosophy and Theology* (Phillipsburg, NJ: P&R, 2015). Included is a short critical analysis of Herman Dooyeweerd and the neo-Kuyperians.

fact especially when they are thinking about modern questions—
they need to take care to root themselves deeply in the details of
Scripture. Scripture is a source for a Christian worldview. But
it is more than mere generalities. It is easy for people who are
philosophically inclined to think that they have enough on which
to build when they have only a few general principles. And then
they go off with these principles to apply themselves to the modern
questions. But principles that are too general do not by themselves
root out all the sinful infestations in the life of the mind. We need
the full texture of Scripture to continue to work in us.

So we have here the beginnings of another principle, namely,
that Scripture itself should play a central and critical role in the
life of the mind. We should use Scripture in that role, rather than
being content merely with a general philosophical distillation of a
few main themes of Scripture.

Two simplistic alternatives. A third and fourth path for dealing with modern life should also be mentioned briefly. The third
is withdrawal. The life of the Amish people in the United States is
an example. They have their own culture and their own schools.
Most of them steer away from any kind of learning except what
has practical benefits for their life. They have let many aspects of
modern life pass them by because they want to maintain their own
communal life and their own commitment to holiness. But their
understanding of holiness is narrow. They may not recognize that
Christians who engage the modern world more vigorously may be
serving Christ faithfully.

The fourth path is to search for specific verses in Scripture
that directly address modern issues. For example, some people
have seen a piece of modern cosmology in Isaiah 44:24, which
says that the Lord "stretched out the heavens." According to their
interpretation, texts like this one refer to the expansion of the universe after the Big Bang. Now the Lord indeed is sovereign over all
the processes that may have been involved in the creation of the
universe. But this particular verse in Isaiah is not talking *directly*

about modern cosmological theories; it is providing a poetic image of God's effortless control, using an analogy with a human being stretching out a tent cover. We see the poetic image more clearly in the parallelism of another verse:

> [The Lord] stretches out the heavens like a *curtain*,
>   and spreads them like a *tent* to dwell in. (Isa. 40:22)

The aforementioned phrase in Isaiah 44:24, "who alone stretched out the heavens," also has a parallel poetic line, which says "who spread out the earth by myself." It is poetry, not scientific cosmology.

Thus, people easily create artificial meanings when they search for individual verses with direct modern reference points. Such a search does not recognize the full texture of Scripture, according to which individual verses contribute to a larger picture rather than functioning primarily in an isolated way to address directly this or that modern issue.

Van Tilian Apologetics

Another resource for the Kuyperian project is Van Tilian apologetics. I indicated earlier that Cornelius Van Til can be classified as one of the successors of Kuyper. He had cordial relations with the neo-Kuyperians at an early point, but later became critical and moved in his own distinctive direction. Van Til taught apologetics and systematic theology at Westminster Theological Seminary for most of his career.

What about apologetics? How do we conduct apologetics if we take seriously the radical antithesis between Christian and non-Christian ways of thinking? Kuyper had virtually rejected the idea of apologetics because he thought it began by conceding too much to non-Christian thought. Van Til found a way of holding Kuyper's view of antithesis and yet developing apologetics as a positive approach.

I must leave it to other works to expound in detail Van Til's rich contributions to apologetics, in addition to systematic theology.[8] But it is worthwhile to note a few points here. Apologetics reflects on how we who are Christians address people who do not hold our commitments. Van Til's insights can bear fruit far beyond the distinct discipline of apologetics because they give us insights on how to conduct our lives. We serve Christ while interacting with others; we act in a world where people have many underlying religious commitments. Christ is Lord in all the world and every distinct situation. But not all people acknowledge his lordship. Therefore, in every sphere we have to deal with the antithesis of basic commitments. Van Til's approach to apologetics emphasized the antithesis. He developed ways of thinking that enable us to analyze more deeply the points of failure in views originating from the unbelieving world.

We also need to deal with common grace. It was a repeated theme in Van Til's writings, and he wrote a whole book on the subject.[9] We can seek opportunities to display love, compassion, grace, and truth to non-Christians as we work in common projects and discuss differences and sometimes also directly oppose evil actions. The situations of dialog are opportunities to use apologetic insights.

It is a great challenge. There is always room for us to grow in understanding and skill in how we interact with others. Van Til has helped me personally as I have endeavored to look with discernment at various issues in biblical studies and hermeneutics, as well as other academic fields. The ideas of antithesis and common grace run through every area of academic life. When Van Til is understood and appreciated, he can powerfully help others in the Kuyperian project.

---

[8] Cornelius Van Til, *The Defense of the Faith*, 4th ed., ed. K. Scott Oliphint (Phillipsburg, NJ: P&R, 2008); Greg L. Bahnsen, *Van Til's Apologetic: Readings and Analysis* (Phillipsburg, NJ: P&R, 1998); John M. Frame, *Apologetics: A Justification of Christian Belief*, 2nd ed. (Phillipsburg, NJ: P&R, 2015); Frame, *Cornelius Van Til: An Analysis of His Thought* (Phillipsburg, NJ: P&R, 1995); Frame, *Van Til the Theologian* (Phillipsburg, NJ: Pilgrim, 1976).

[9] Cornelius Van Til, *Common Grace and the Gospel* (Nutley, NJ: Presbyterian and Reformed, 1972); see also William D. Dennison, "Van Til and Common Grace," *Mid-America Journal of Theology* 9 (1993): 225–47.

Multiple Perspectives

Another resource for serving Christ in all of life is the use of multiple perspectives. In one sense, multiple perspectives are commonplace. Wherever we have multiple people, we have multiple perspectives. And when people interact, they may enrich one another, as each person listens carefully to the other person's perspective. But, contrary to some postmodernist thinking, an appreciation for multiple perspectives need not mean that we affirm contradictory ideas. To value another person and his perspective does not mean that we affirm that his ideas are true. Nor does it mean—as sometimes one hears in postmodernist circles—that what is true for me can be *not* true for you, or vice versa.

We ought to believe in absolute truth—the truth of God, such as he reveals to us through Scripture. At the same time, we can say that each of us has a personal perspective on the truths that he knows. We must endeavor to appreciate multiple perspectives and also to appreciate absolute truth. The appropriate model for this kind of interaction is found in the body of Christ. According to 1 Corinthians 12, the church is the body of Christ; it is one body with many members. The different members have different functions. They work together, and when the body is healthy, each member contributes to the health and well-being of the other members. This interaction includes interaction in knowledge. When someone else teaches you a truth that you did not know before, you grow in knowledge. Likewise, if you correct someone else's error and he receives the correction graciously, you help him grow in knowledge.[10]

How would the use of multiple perspectives help in serving

---

[10] One may find a fuller exposition of ideas about multiple perspectives in writings by John M. Frame and me, and others who appear in the Festschrift dedicated to John Frame (John J. Hughes, ed., *Speaking the Truth in Love: The Theology of John M. Frame* [Phillipsburg, NJ: P&R, 2009]). See especially Vern S. Poythress, *Symphonic Theology: The Validity of Multiple Perspectives in Theology* (repr., Phillipsburg, NJ: P&R, 2001); John M. Frame, "A Primer on Perspectivalism," 2008, accessed July 14, 2014, http://www.frame-poythress.org/a-primer-on-perspectivalism/; Frame, *The Doctrine of the Knowledge of God* (Phillipsburg, NJ: Presbyterian and Reformed, 1987); and Frame, *Perspectives on the Word of God: An Introduction to Christian Ethics* (Eugene, OR: Wipf & Stock, 1999).

Christ in all of life? The point made earlier about the differences between the cultures of the Bible and modern cultures applies here. It is sometimes hard for modern readers to see the relevance of the Bible, especially beyond the area of church worship, individual emotional life, and family life. Using multiple perspectives in examining the Bible can help us to make significant connections with the present. And using multiple perspectives on the present can help us to see the present in the light of scriptural teaching.

We can again use science as an illustration. Mainstream biologists customarily look at biology as reducible to chemistry and to gradualistic evolutionary explanations. But we can look at life as a divine wonder that shows control, purpose, design, and analogy—all derivative from God.[11] A practice of self-consciously looking at the phenomena of life through multiple perspectives can help to make us aware of how impoverished a purely materialistic approach is and of where reductionism fails in its details.

Awareness of multiple perspectives can also help us as we undertake the difficult task of sorting out what is good and bad, what is true and untrue, in the culture around us. We should endeavor both to listen carefully to another person's perspective and to bring it into critical relationship to Christian teaching given to us in the Bible. That is what the proper kind of multiperspectivalism is about.

Finally, we may note that the use of multiple perspectives relates comfortably to biblical theology. The multiple themes in the Bible become one focus of biblical theology. We may study what the Bible says about the theme of the glory of God, the theme of the justice of God, the theme of God's dwelling in the tabernacle and the temple, the theme of God's covenants with mankind, the theme of God's kingly rule, the theme of priesthood, and so on. We quickly see that these themes intersect one another and interlock with one another in rich ways. They are not strictly isolated from

---

[11] Poythress, *Redeeming Science*, chaps. 17–19.

each other. They easily get turned into *perspectives* on the whole of Scripture. So they become one important way in which we can not only listen to the perspective of another person but also listen successively to multiple perspectives found in the multiple biblical-theological themes in Scripture. In doing this kind of listening, we are using multiple perspectives as an important tool to understand Scripture more deeply and apply it more discerningly.

Part 3

AREAS OF SERVICE

10

Christ the Lord of
Life and Religion

Now we may explore how Christ's lordship has implications for various spheres of life. We take our start from the way Abraham Kuyper probed the implications in the six chapters of his seminal book *Lectures on Calvinism*:[1]

1. Calvinism a Life-system
2. Calvinism and Religion
3. Calvinism and Politics
4. Calvinism and Science
5. Calvinism and Art
6. Calvinism and the Future

Readers can still profit from reading the original lectures, delivered at Princeton Seminary. But over a century has gone by since they were given. So it seems useful to add some comment to what Kuyper said.

First, let us consider the topics in the first two chapters of Kuyper's book, on a "life-system" and "religion."

---

[1] Abraham Kuyper, *Lectures on Calvinism: Six Lectures Delivered at Princeton University under Auspices of the L. P. Stone Foundation* (Grand Rapids, MI: Eerdmans, 1931).

The "Life-System"

Commitment to Christ affects all of life. Kuyper's first chapter, "Calvinism a Life-system," makes the point that Calvinism at its root contains ideas about God, man, and the world that lead to vigorous developments in life and culture.[2] Such convictions spring to life in human hearts because the Holy Spirit works redemption in human beings through the power of Christ and through the power of his word in Scripture. God reigns over all nations. His rule over history includes redemptive transformation of human beings through Christ. As people are transformed, their cultures likewise undergo change.

Change takes place through the rule of Christ, who is now Lord of all. And one of the means that God has ordained to effect change is the process of our coming to understand the greatness of Christ. Deep knowledge of his greatness energizes our affections, our thoughts, and our actions. Christ's lordship has implications for the totality of a person's life, as we began to see in earlier chapters.

Redemption

Christ's redemption sets in motion many changes in human beings. In this connection, the words *redeem* and *redemption* can be used narrowly or broadly. Used narrowly, they refer to the redemption that Christ accomplished once and for all. This redemption is now being applied to individuals. But the language of redemption also applies to the church, which is the body of Christ, the society of redeemed individuals. In other words, God has redeemed both individuals and the entire people of God at one time, through the death and resurrection of Christ. But this one redemption is applied throughout all times.

---

[2] Kuyper's chapter also includes speculation about phases of historical development for the whole human race. But speculation is just that. We must anchor our hopes in the promises of God and in the sovereign work of God. We depend on the work of God to bring about new life for each new human being who comes into the world in his first birth (Ps. 139:13–17) and for each new regenerate person who is born again by the Holy Spirit (John 3:1–16). It is God who must energize those who bring about social change.

God's redemptive transformation of individuals leads also to changes in families, in social relationships, in education, and in many other spheres. The people who are redeemed begin to live differently, and the way they live changes every area of their lives. For example, since the work of God transforms our minds (Rom. 12:1–2), it influences how we think about various areas of science and humanities and technology and work and entertainment.

This change in living leads to the possibility of a *broad* use of the words *redeem* and *redemption*. Can we speak of *redeeming* our thinking? In a narrow sense, only human beings are redeemed. Thinking itself cannot be redeemed except tangentially, through the redemption of those who are changed by the Holy Spirit. It might be safer to speak only about human thinking "changing" or undergoing "transformation" or being "reformed." Romans 12:2 speaks about being "*transformed* by the *renewal* of your mind." But by themselves, words like *change, transform, reform,* and *renew* do not explicitly express the fact that these changes are not made in a vacuum. At their best, they are brought about because of the effects of Christ's redemption within human beings.

So how do we describe such changes in a way that explicitly acknowledges that all the glory belongs to Christ and to his accomplished redemption? One way would be to use the word *redemption* in a broader sense. We say that human thinking is being "redeemed." With this label, we are reminding ourselves that these healthy and godly changes in thinking have come about only because of the merits of Christ's redemption. They come about as further effects, based on the fact that Christ has redeemed the human beings who do the thinking.

The disadvantage of this label is that we may be tempted to think that these changes somehow *supplement* the work of Christ. We would then falsely imply that we ourselves are little autonomous "redeemers," co-redeemers alongside Christ, rather than Christ being the one Redeemer, the "one mediator between God and men" (1 Tim. 2:5). We must make sure that all the glory goes to Christ. We are servants through whom Christ may be pleased to show his glory by bringing transformation and healing, based on his unique redemption, accomplished once and for all.

Consider an example. Suppose the Jones family become Christian believers. The husband and wife and children have individually been redeemed. That is redemption in the narrow sense. Strictly speaking, in the narrow sense the family as such is not redeemed; the individual members are.

But, more broadly, we may speak of the "redemption" of family life when the husband and wife and children begin more and more to practice Christian love toward others in the family. They ask for forgiveness and receive it from each other. If one member of the family does not become a Christian while all the others do, the family as a whole still undergoes redemptive transformation under the influence of the work of the Holy Spirit in the lives of the believing family members. Christ has brought about these changes. The glory goes to him.

Moreover, the unbeliever within the family still experiences change. If he is honest, he has to admit that the family is looking different. And it looks different in Christlike ways—ways that reflect the love and glory of Christ. But that by itself does not produce salvation in the unbelieving member. Unless he is convicted of his sin and repents, he is still just as unredeemed as he ever was. In fact, he is *more* guilty, because he has hardened his heart, even after hearing about Christ from the rest of the family and seeing the Christlike love displayed among them.

The distinction between broad and narrow senses is pertinent when we consider our hope for the new heaven and new earth, mentioned in Revelation 21:1. In this new world, will there be "redeemed" families? It depends on what we mean. All the saved individuals in the Jones family will be there. But if any member remains unsaved, he will not. That is the narrow sense of redemption as it applies to individuals and to the church. But what about the broad sense, in which the changes in individuals lead to changes in family interaction? In the new world, the idea of family itself gets altered, because in the new world "they neither marry nor are given in marriage, but are like angels in heaven" (Matt. 22:30). The whole of the new humanity is the "family" of God, but that involves a different meaning. The redeemed members of the Jones family will be practicing perfectly the love that they already show to one another on earth imperfectly.

Religion

Kuyper's vision for Christ as Lord of all fits together with an understanding of the nature of religion. Every human being is innately religious because he lives in the presence of God and is responsible to God. Every human being is either regenerate or unregenerate. He is either following God or in rebellion against God. Both stances come from the heart. A person either loves God or hates him (Luke 16:13). In these words we are re-expressing the principle of antithesis. But, as usual, we need to acknowledge the presence of common grace in unbelievers. And we acknowledge the presence of remaining sin in believers. So real people act in mixed ways.

How will we describe this situation? How will we use the word *religion*? The term can be used in more than one way. In one kind of use, it evokes distinctively "religious" practices of worship: religious rituals, prayer or meditation, the study of texts that people regard as holy. Such practices occur in false religions as well as in true service to the true God. "Religion" encompasses distinctive practices that people use in hope of accessing a world of spirits or something holy. These practices are often set apart from the rest of life, with the sense that they belong to a "holy" sphere.

Most traditional religions have some such practices. Animists may consult shamans or offer sacrifices to propitiate spirits. Hindus offer sacrifices in their temples. Modern Jews assemble on the Sabbath to hear the Torah read and to sing religious songs. Muslims and Christians may have special times set apart for prayer, as well as large meetings one day a week (Friday for Muslims, Sunday for Christians). Agnostics, atheists, and people of a secular bent do nothing of this kind. They are in this sense not "religious" people.

But in another sense whatever holds a person's deepest commitment is his "religion." If a person's deepest commitment is to a personal God or gods, his commitment is likely to express itself partly in traditional, distinctive religious practices. On the other hand, a person's deepest commitment may be to atheism, in which case atheism is his "religion." Or, without consciously having a commitment to believing or disbelieving in God, a person can serve money or sex or pleasure or power as his deepest commitment. Whatever he is committed to functions like a god. Money becomes a god to a person who lusts for money and consumes his life in the single-minded pursuit of it. Money is his "religion" in this expanded sense.

This larger sense of "religion" is useful because God—the real God described in the Bible—cares about ultimate allegiances. We have already reflected on the greatest commandment, "You shall love the Lord your God with all your heart and with all your soul and with all your mind" (Matt. 22:37). If you are *not* loving God with all your heart, you are loving something else with at least part of your heart. And often there rises up something in particular that captures a person's primary allegiance. That something is his substitute for God. It is a little god. And the service to that little god contradicts God's commandment to worship him alone: "You shall have no other gods before me" (Ex. 20:3).

The Kuyperians therefore developed the motto "Life is religion." They were pointing to this issue of ultimate allegiance. They were telling us to observe that in all human action, we are serving *something*. We have a goal, perhaps a short-range goal. But behind the short-range goal is a deeper and more ultimate desire. Our hearts were made by God to find satisfaction in knowing and loving God, and in receiving his love. But if we flee from God, our hearts are hungry. We will serve something. And whatever that something is, it deeply affects the direction of our action. Our motivations matter, even if at times other people cannot see them.

This understanding of life as religion goes together with the principle of the absolute sovereignty of God and his presence in all the world. Service to God belongs not merely to a narrow sphere of specific ritualistic practices, but to all of life, because in all of life God is present to us, and we are open to the inspection of his holy gaze.

This insight into life as religion also shows how desperately guilty we are before God. We have not just sinned here and there or in outward ways. We have idolatrous hearts. We are deeply guilty. We need Christ to take away our guilt through justification and to renew our hearts through the work of the Holy Spirit.

11

Politics

Kuyper was heavily involved in politics in his own day, and it is natural that he should take up that topic in his key book *Lectures on Calvinism* (chap. 3).[1] Working for changes in the political sphere was important for him because he thought that civil government was under the universal lordship of Christ. He also saw that Christian living could proceed with freedom only if the civil government protected religious liberty.

The Principle of Limited Authority

Following Scripture, Kuyper believed in the absolute sovereignty of God. That implied that the authority of civil government was limited by God. Ideas coming out of the French Revolution treated the state as if it were god walking on earth. It was given unlimited sovereignty. Kuyper, by contrast, saw that the state has genuine authority, but only such authority as has been delegated by God: "Let every person be subject to the governing authorities. For there is no authority except *from God*, and those that exist have been *instituted by God*" (Rom. 13:1). These principles have

---

[1] Abraham Kuyper, *Lectures on Calvinism: Six Lectures Delivered at Princeton University under Auspices of the L. P. Stone Foundation* (Grand Rapids, MI: Eerdmans, 1931).

definite implications for politics. Both the intrinsic limitation of state authority and the superiority of divine authority function to check the danger of tyranny and despotism.

The Principle of Equity

Kuyper believed that civil government should maintain and promote *equity*. Unlike some of the earlier generations of European Christians, and unlike some of his own contemporaries, Kuyper rightly saw that equity with respect to religion meant not favoring any one religion. The government should not favor the Christian religion or the Christian church over the Jews, and it should not favor Protestants over Catholics. Neither should it favor the modern substitutes for traditional religion—atheism, humanism, and secularism. Kuyper argued that this principle had implications for education as well as for freedom of association in other types of organization.

Churches, synagogues, temples, and other religious institutions all had a right to exist. They had a right to equal protection by civil law. No particular institution should be favored over another, either with special legal privileges or with special subsidies.

In addition, since all education is religiously grounded and not religiously neutral, people of all convictions and commitments should have an equal right to maintain and use educational institutions that aligned with their commitments. "Secular" schools must be on the same footing as "religious" schools. If one kind were to be supported by government funding, they must all be equally supported. This kind of thinking was one impetus behind Kuyper's step of founding the Free University of Amsterdam based specifically on Reformed religious commitment.

The Relevance of Scripture

As we have seen, Kuyper drew fundamental insights from Scripture about divine sovereignty and state authority. At its core, his thinking followed scriptural principles about authority. But when we look in more detail, Kuyper's arguments depended in addition on very general principles concerning the nature of religion, the nature of civil government, and the nature of society. It is not always clear what is the ground for his principles. Are they grounded in philosophical intuition about the nature of justice and the state? Intuitions can be valuable, but they are not an ultimate source of authority. Are they grounded in Scripture? Maybe so, but the path from Scripture to political principle is not always clearly demarcated in Kuyper's writings.[2]

With John Frame[3] and others in the Reformed tradition, I believe that Scripture articulates the fullness of our ethical obligations to God and man. The Westminster Confession of Faith summarizes:

> The *whole* counsel of God concerning *all things* necessary for His own glory, man's salvation, faith and *life*, is either expressly set down in Scripture, or by good and necessary consequence may be deduced from Scripture: unto which *nothing* at any time is to be added, whether by new revelations of the Spirit or *traditions* of men.[4]

This principle follows from the fact that God is the source for all sound moral principles and has fully articulated our responsibilities to him in Scripture. One indication of the sufficiency of Scripture lies in Psalm 119:1:

> Blessed are those whose way is *blameless*,
> who walk in the law of the LORD!

This verse implies that if you want to be blameless, you only need to "walk in the law of the LORD." You do not need to do anything more. Of course that is not easy! In fact, it is impossible to do

---

[2] See Klaas Schilder, *Christ and Culture*, trans. G. van Rongen and W. Helder (Winnipeg: Premier, 1977), 13–14; online with different pagination, accessed February 6, 2015, http://www.reformed .org/webfiles/cc/christ_and_culture.pdf, 14–15.
[3] John M. Frame, *The Doctrine of the Christian Life* (Phillipsburg, NJ: P&R, 2008).
[4] Westminster Confession of Faith 1.6, italics mine.

fully in our state of sin. The law of the Lord is deep and challenging. The two great commandments, the commandment to love God and to love one's neighbor (Matt. 22:37–40), are exceedingly deep. Jesus Christ kept the law perfectly, but no one else on earth does. Nevertheless, Psalm 119:1 does indicate that the law of the Lord is sufficient to instruct us in our duty.

The Sufficiency of Scripture for Ethics (Including Political Ethics)

The principle of the *sufficiency of Scripture* implies that Scripture does not need supplementation via fundamental ethical principles that come from elsewhere. Yes, the principles of Scripture have to be *applied* to our situation, and this step of application may be difficult. When we are led by the Holy Spirit, our intuitions can help us at times to notice scriptural principles that we might otherwise overlook. But we ought not to bind people's consciences to *further* principles that we derive from another source—even if that source is alleged to be general revelation or sanctified intuition. Again, the Westminster Confession of Faith is pertinent: "God alone is Lord of the conscience, and hath left it *free* from the doctrines and commandments of men, which are, in any thing, contrary to His Word; or beside it, if matters of faith, or worship."[5]

The confession goes on to say that we should submit to lawful authority (which would include officers of civil government, but also parents, employers, and so on).[6] But those whom God has placed in authority should not exceed their authority by ordering things contrary to God's Word, or by imposing extra requirements beyond Scripture in matters of faith and worship.

Sometimes it takes great discernment to apply scriptural principles to specific situations. Christians may disagree with one another. We need to exercise charity when disagreements arise in

---

[5] Ibid., 20.2, italics mine.
[6] Ibid., 20.4.

difficult areas. Parents need wisdom in raising their children, and governing authorities need wisdom in making good laws. But the general principle still holds: we do not need to add man-made moral principles to Scripture in order to follow God's way fully.

General revelation from God includes revelation of the character of God through the world he has made (Rom. 1:19–21) and revelation of the character of God through human beings themselves, who are made in the image of God. As one aspect of this revelation, human conscience has a sense of right and wrong (Rom. 1:32). This moral sense comes from God. But it can be distorted and in fact *is* distorted by sin. And Scripture never suggests that the promptings of conscience are more complete, let alone more accurate, than the ethical instruction of Scripture itself.

How to Use Scripture for Politics

Thus, we can deepen and enhance our understanding of justice and the principles for civil government by using biblical theology to examine biblical teaching concerning topics related to politics.

It is challenging to study Scripture from a political point of view. How do we do it? We could focus first of all on the rich biblical teaching about the rule and kingship of God. This teaching is indeed most important. It comes to fulfillment and focus in the universal lordship of Christ. We then ask, what implications does Christ's kingship and lordship have for political questions?

We can see that human kings and governors have their authority from God, and that they should imitate the rule of God. But in what ways specifically? The major difficulty here is that human authority is *analogous* to divine kingship; but an analogy is not an identity. Human authorities are like God in some ways, and unlike him in other ways. In order to have specific guidance for our thinking, we must attend not only to teaching about God's kingship but also to teaching specifically focused on human authorities. Moreover, the human authorities are of several kinds. Parents have authority over their children, and kings have authority over their subjects. Not everything about authority is pertinent to each particular *kind* of authority.

In many places the Bible articulates principles of justice that pertain to civil government. But the New Testament passages that directly address the issue are relatively few (Matt. 22:15–22 and the parallel passages in Mark 12:13–17 and Luke 20:19–26; Rom. 13:1–7; 1 Pet. 2:13–17).[7]

The Old Testament has many passages about the Israelite kings and their practices, and many passages from the Mosaic law that are relevant directly or indirectly to the practice of justice and the responsibilities of civil government. God gave his instructions both to the judges who had governing responsibility and to the people who were under the authority of the judges. But there are difficulties in applying these passages. To understand them, we have to consider the context in which God gave them. The Old Testament instructions were part of a development in the history of redemption leading to Christ. Not everything was intended by God to be permanent.

In particular, the instructions about governing responsibilities in the Mosaic period came in the context of the fact that God had chosen Israel to be a holy nation: "Now therefore, if you will indeed obey my voice and keep my covenant, you shall be my treasured possession among all peoples, for all the earth is mine; and you shall be to me a *kingdom of priests and a holy nation.* These are the words that you shall speak to the people of Israel" (Ex. 19:5–6).

Israel as a holy nation had a special obligation to maintain its holiness. That is why the people were told not to tolerate false religion in their midst (Deut. 7:1–5; 13:1–18). That status of holiness was unique to Israel and did not belong to any other nation. Moreover, the symbolic holiness of Israel was a temporary provision in the history of redemption. The holiness of Israel was

---

[7] The book of Revelation is relevant because of the relation of the figure of the Beast (Rev. 13:1–8) to the power of the state.

a shadow or symbol pointing forward to the holiness of Christ, who is the true Israel, the true Son of God. Christ's holiness in turn gets reflected in the people of Christ, who are called saints ("holy ones," 1 Cor. 1:2; 3:17). Such holiness does not belong to the Roman emperor or any office of modern civil government. Thus, the provisions made for Israel have lessons for us. But they are lessons expressed in symbolic form. And the lessons concerning holiness are relevant to the church as the holy people of God, rather than to the modern state.

Consider, for example the pattern of destroying idolatrous practices in the land of Israel (Deuteronomy 13). This pattern is a shadow pointing toward the zeal of Christ's holiness. And from there it comes to be applied to the church, which should maintain holiness and expel the unholy, unrepentant person from its midst by excommunication (1 Cor. 5:5, 13).

Excommunication is a solemn act by which the church declares that the excommunicated person is subject to *spiritual* death. The church still prays for repentance to take place in that person. And if he repents, he is forgiven by Christ and restored to the community (2 Cor. 2:7–11). The process of excommunication—and possible restoration—is the true fulfillment of the Old Testament laws against idolatry. It was a terrible mistake when in past generations in Europe, people who professed to be Christians undertook to use the *civil government* to exterminate idolatry and heresy. After praying and urging idolaters and heretics to repent, *the church* must expel the unrepentant. The civil government must treat them in accordance with God's principles of equity that apply to this government. It does not punish idolatry and heresy, but it does punish crimes against fellow human beings, such as murder and theft.

At the same time, the Old Testament law of Moses embodies and illustrates principles of equity that apply today. That is why modern governments still undertake to restrain and punish murderers and thieves, and should continue to do so.

So in the Old Testament, how do we separate permanent principles of equity from special principles for Israel as a holy people?[8] It is not easy. But it is important that we attempt it. Otherwise, our modern political notions and intuitions, which have been shaped partly by modern secular ideals, are likely to influence us. If we are swayed by modern ideals, we proceed to formulate out of our own minds very general principles for justice or for the nature of the state, and we infer applications to various political problems. We end up being guided primarily by a political *philosophy*, whose motivations and origins are difficult to discern, rather than by the word of God, speaking to us in Scripture.[9]

Biblical Theology

Accordingly, we need to engage in a biblical-theological analysis of scriptural teaching, with a view to finding its implications for the principles of civil justice, statecraft, and the structures and authorities in society.[10] This work is fallible, but it can be a useful supplement to and deepening of Kuyper's work in seeking to submit politics and political thinking to the lordship of Christ.

---

[8] The Westminster Confession of Faith recognizes the distinction: "To them [Israel] also, as a body *politic*, He gave sundry judicial laws, which *expired* together with the State of that people; not obliging any other now, further than the *general equity* thereof may require" (19.4, italics mine). But in its original form the Westminster Confession of Faith itself did not work out fully the principles of equity (23.3).

[9] That does not mean that distorted political philosophies or other distorted ideas never have an influence on the modern interpretations of Scripture. Of course they may. But at least Scripture itself offers resistance to such distortions. By contrast, when philosophy or political ideals are shaped without reference to Scripture, the distortions are likely to have freer rein.

[10] See Vern S. Poythress, *The Shadow of Christ in the Law of Moses* (repr., Phillipsburg, NJ: P&R, 1995), esp. part 2, "Understanding Specific Penalties of the Law"; Poythress, *Redeeming Sociology: A God-Centered Approach* (Wheaton, IL: Crossway, 2011), esp. chaps. 25–27.

12

Science

When Kuyper took up the topic of science in *Lectures on Calvinism* (chap. 4),[1] he used the word *science* with a broad meaning. He meant "learning, knowledge, scholarship" or "academic disciplines," in line with the broad meaning of key words in Dutch (*wetenschap*) and German (*Wissenschaft*).[2] Under this broad meaning Kuyper included natural sciences, but also social sciences and humanities. Kuyper maintained that Christ is Lord of all knowledge and thus is Lord over every academic sphere and all academic studies.

Natural Science

Since the natural sciences are included under Christ's lordship, we may begin with them. Natural sciences are an important area for several reasons.

(1) Science has wide cultural impact. (2) There is a naive but widespread idea that science and Christian faith are in conflict. Because of the prevalence of this idea, science becomes a secular-

---

[1] Abraham Kuyper, *Lectures on Calvinism: Six Lectures Delivered at Princeton University under Auspices of the L. P. Stone Foundation* (Grand Rapids, MI: Eerdmans, 1931).
[2] Ibid., 112.

izing force. (3) The successes of science have made it attractive for some people to treat it as a model for the meanings and methods necessary for knowledge in any sphere. (4) It is often thought that science operates in an atmosphere of religious neutrality. (5) The idea of a mechanical universe, based on Newtonian physics, is used as a platform for materialism or deistic philosophy. (6) Darwinian evolution is used to support the case for atheism. (7) The specialized research and specialized theories in science are unique to the modern era, giving the superficial impression that the Bible can have nothing relevant to say about science. (8) Since Kuyper's day there have been faulty attempts by some Christian believers to read scientific detail into the Bible, and to show that a particular verse remarkably anticipates some piece of detailed scientific theory. It is wisest to answer such attempts not merely by refuting misinterpretations of the Bible but by developing a positive Christian view of the nature of science and its role in human life and human knowledge.

Kuyper's Contribution

In his own day, Kuyper undertook to develop a distinctively Christian approach to science. It remains to us to continue his line of thinking, rather than merely capitulating to a status-quo view of what science is, how it works, and what its place is in society.

Areas for Exploration

So what issues need to be explored? It is always appropriate to return to issues about the foundation of science, and to inspect critically what assumptions are contributing to that foundation. In addition, as was suggested in chapter 9, biblical theology can make a contribution. It can help by encouraging us to be anchored directly in biblical teaching, rather than only making use of high-level philosophical and theological generalizations about the nature of the world—the nature of nature, if you will.

One important theme for biblical theological exploration is the theme of God's speech governing the universe. As I indicated in chapter 9, that theme has immediate relevance for how we understand the nature of scientific law. When scientists investigate scientific laws, they are studying God's speech governing the universe.

But other themes may also be useful. For example, we can look at the theme of human dominion in the Bible. Science is the work of human beings, who are made in the image of God and who are descendants of Adam. The initial task of dominion given to mankind in the beginning (Gen. 1:28–30) includes many aspects. Dominion includes understanding God's governance of the world. Such understanding leads to science. Dominion also includes the use of our understanding in order to enhance the glory of the world that God gave us. So dominion leads to technology. Science and technology can be used in selfish and exploitive ways. And since sin has come into the human race through Adam, we do see corrupt uses of science and technology. But through Scripture we can also see that the original design of God for creation involved a positive task for human beings. And this task is reiterated after the fall in Genesis 9:2–3. Science and technology are intrinsically good and honorable things. The tragedy is that sin corrupts them, as it corrupts every area of human life and every aspect of human relationships to the rest of creation.

Christ came to earth to accomplish redemption. Through his redemption he triumphed over sin and death and corruption. He came as "the last Adam" (1 Cor. 15:45). He achieved what Adam failed to achieve. This achievement has universal relevance and transforms our view of the task of modern science. We need to explore what the Bible says about Christ's exaltation, his role as the last Adam, and his fulfillment of the mandate of dominion given to the human race in Genesis 1:28.[3] Scientists who are Christian believers should conduct their scientific work in union with Christ the Lord, who has full wisdom and has achieved full dominion.

---

[3] See Vern S. Poythress, *Redeeming Science: A God-Centered Approach* (Wheaton, IL: Crossway, 2006), chaps. 11–12.

There are still other themes to explore in biblical theology. The theme of imaging, developed in Meredith G. Kline's book *Images of the Spirit*,[4] is relevant because it has thematic connections with the whole area of physical display, and from there we can see further analogies with investigations in natural science.[5] The theme of life in the Bible is frequently related to the promise of *eternal life* given in Christ. But the theme goes back to creation. God is the *living* God. When God created *living things*, he created life that was on the level of creatures but still analogous to his own original uncreated life. Living things display his glory. They are not merely bags of chemicals.

Social Sciences

Similar principles hold with respect to the social sciences. The theme of God's speech governing the universe is pertinent to social sciences as well as natural science. God rules not only over the physical world but also over the social world.

> For his dominion is an everlasting dominion,
>   and his kingdom endures from generation to generation;
> all the inhabitants of the earth are accounted as nothing,
>   and he does according to his will among the host of
>   heaven
>   and among the inhabitants of the earth;
> and none can stay his hand
>   or say to him, "What have you done?" (Dan. 4:34–35)

> The LORD has made everything for its purpose,
>   even the wicked for the day of trouble.
> Everyone who is arrogant in heart is an abomination to
>   the LORD;
>   be assured, he will not go unpunished.
> By steadfast love and faithfulness iniquity is atoned for,

---

[4] Meredith G. Kline, *Images of the Spirit* (Grand Rapids, MI: Baker, 1980).
[5] Poythress, *Redeeming Science*, chaps. 20–22.

and by the fear of the LORD one turns away from evil.
When a man's ways please the LORD,
  he makes even his enemies to be at peace with him.
Better is a little with righteousness
  than great revenues with injustice.
The heart of man plans his way,
  but the LORD establishes his steps. (Prov. 16:4–9)

The Lord's rule over the social world has pertinence to how social scientists view the whole object of their study. Do they view the human social world as self-contained or as continuously under the care of God and open to the active rule of God?

In addition, various themes in the Bible have pertinence to particular subdivisions within social science. For example, in the Bible God's speech is the original speech, of which human speech is an imitation. This insight has an effect on how we conceive of *linguistics*. Christ's redemption includes, as one of its effects, the overcoming of linguistic barriers (Acts 2:5–11). This insight influences how we think about translation and the challenge of linguistic barriers in our day.[6]

Consider also the subject of social relationships. The eternal relation between the Father and the Son and the Holy Spirit in the Trinity is the original personal relationship. God in creating human beings ordained the patterns of human relationship. Among these relationships is the relation of father and son. It is obviously a creaturely relationship, but it is modeled after the eternal relationship between God the Father and God the Son. Relationships of love among human beings are modeled after the eternal love among the persons of the Trinity.

God's Trinitarian nature is not only a *model* but also a source of power and sustenance of these relationships. Relationships arise among human beings according to the plan of God the Father, through the speech of God in his Son, in the power of the Holy

---

[6] Vern S. Poythress, *In the Beginning Was the Word: Language—A God-Centered Approach* (Wheaton, IL: Crossway, 2009).

Spirit. The Holy Spirit is present in order to empower us to love. These insights have an influence on how we conceive of human family relationships, and then more broadly on how we conceive of any social relationships. Christ's redemption results in the healing of personal relationships, both between God and man and among human beings. So his redemption should inform how we think about the healing of social relationships, including the overcoming of ethnic barriers and ethnic prejudice.[7]

The Bible also has themes that address concerns in psychology. The Bible's teaching that man is made in the image of God informs what we think human nature is. The Bible's teaching about sin and redemption informs how we go about addressing human psychological struggles.[8]

---

[7] Vern S. Poythress, *Redeeming Sociology: A God-Centered Approach* (Wheaton, IL: Crossway, 2011).

[8] David Powlison, *Seeing with New Eyes: Counseling and the Human Condition through the Lens of Scripture* (Phillipsburg, NJ: P&R, 2003); Powlison, *The Biblical Counseling Movement: History and Context* (Greensboro, NC: New Growth, 2010); James MacDonald, ed., *Christ-Centered Biblical Counseling* (Eugene, OR: Harvest House, 2013).

13

Art

The topic of art, Kuyper's fifth chapter in *Lectures on Calvinism*,[1] is significant because too many Christians view art as a dispensable part of their experience, a superficial decoration added to the activities at the core of life. Since Kuyper's day, art has grown in cultural importance and influence through the expression of artistic excellence in communications, media, advertising, and entertainment (particularly movies and songs). Popular artistic expressions have an influence on culture that may equal or exceed the influence of formal education.

For one thing, artistic expression can affect our imaginations. And we are arguably motivated as much by what we imagine as by rational inference. Will that motivation reinforce Christian ethics and Christian living or undermine it?

Not everyone is equally gifted in the arts. But whether we are interested or not, gifted or not, we need to take to heart Kuyper's concern for the importance of art and to encourage those who are more gifted.

Once again biblical theology offers us avenues for exploring themes in the Bible related to art. The Old Testament prophets

---

[1] Abraham Kuyper, *Lectures on Calvinism: Six Lectures Delivered at Princeton University under Auspices of the L. P. Stone Foundation* (Grand Rapids, MI: Eerdmans, 1931).

and the New Testament book of Revelation both contain many passages and imagistic language that appeal to the heart and to the imagination. They encourage us to move beyond a narrowly intellectual interest in the Bible, and a narrowly intellectual response.

The tabernacle of Moses and the temple of Solomon with their furnishings show great beauty. The instructions for making the priestly garments explicitly say that they are "for glory and for *beauty*" (Ex. 28:2). We know from biblical-theological reflection that the tabernacle and the temple are shadows pointing forward to Christ (John 2:21). The Old Testament priesthood points forward to the final priesthood of Christ (Heb. 4:14–15; 7:1–10:25). Thus, the beauty of the priestly garments points forward to the beauty of Christ. God, as he appears in majesty in Revelation 4, is supremely beautiful in holiness. His beauty is reflected in the things that he has made.[2]

Here we find a supreme motivation for human artistic work: human artists should be growing in the appreciation of the beauty of God and drawing attention to it through their creative work. That does not mean that artists may not concern themselves with ugliness. This world is a fallen world, ruptured by sin. So art can also be used to remind us of what is wrong with the world in order that we may turn to God for the remedy. Art may stimulate us to long for the second coming of Christ and the creation of a new heaven and a new earth (Rev. 21:1).

The theme of creativity also has pertinence. God is the Creator of all. He is the absolute source of creativity. Human beings are made in his image, and so they are derivatively creative.[3] The theme of creativity can be explored in biblical-theological study. Artists should be seeking fellowship with God, because he is the ultimate source for all creativity.

---

[2] Sam Storms, *One Thing: Developing a Passion for the Beauty of God* (Fearn, UK: Christian Focus, 2004), esp. 45–63.

[3] Dorothy L. Sayers, *The Mind of the Maker* (New York: Harcourt, Brace, 1941); Vern S. Poythress, *In the Beginning Was the Word: Language—A God-Centered Approach* (Wheaton, IL: Crossway, 2009), chap. 6.

14

The Future

The final chapter of Kuyper's famous book *Lectures on Calvinism*[1] is about the future, a fitting topic to round out the discussion of the lordship of Christ. Our goal in life should be to bring glory to God, and that means honoring Christ as Lord. Having the goal clearly before us helps not only with our motivations but also with our sense of direction and our decisions along the way.

The Hope of Consummation

Our goal is not only to serve the Lord in this life but also to serve with the hope of future glory in the new heaven and the new earth. We can have communion with Christ in this life through the Holy Spirit. According to Ephesians 1:14, the Holy Spirit is the "guarantee" or "down payment" (ESV margin) of our inheritance. We receive the first portion of our inheritance when we receive the Holy Spirit. We wait for its full realization in the new heaven and the new earth. Biblical theology accordingly speaks of "inaugurated eschatology," the fact that the Old Testament

---

[1] Abraham Kuyper, *Lectures on Calvinism: Six Lectures Delivered at Princeton University under Auspices of the L. P. Stone Foundation* (Grand Rapids, MI: Eerdmans, 1931).

promises concerning the last days have already received inaugural fulfillment in Christ. Theology speaks of two poles: the "already" and the "not yet."

Two Aspects of Inaugurated Eschatology

The two poles are useful as guides in thinking about our service to Christ within this age. Consider, first, the pole of the "already." We ourselves are citizens of heaven (Phil. 3:20) and participants in the "Jerusalem above" (Gal. 4:26). As the Holy Spirit empowers our service, in a fundamental way our service belongs to the new age of the Holy Spirit, the "new creation" inaugurated in Christ (2 Cor. 5:17).

Next, consider the pole of the "not yet." We must not invest hopes merely in this world. Though we serve in the world that God made, and we serve people made in the image of God, 1 Corinthians 7 counsels us not to invest in this world as if it were ultimate:

> This is what I mean, brothers: the appointed time has grown very short. From now on, let those who have wives live as though they had none, and those who mourn as though they were not mourning, and those who rejoice as though they were not rejoicing, and those who buy as though they had no goods, and those who deal with the world as though they had no dealings with it. For the present form of this world is passing away. (1 Cor. 7:29–31)

Measuring Success

We must not measure success by the standards of this world. Does it matter whether we build a powerful organization or achieve remarkable political goals or make a lot of money? It matters only whether we are faithful in serving the Lord.

> It is required of stewards that they be found *faithful*.
> (1 Cor. 4:2)

Whatever you do, work heartily, as *for the Lord* and not for men, knowing that from the Lord you will receive the inheritance as your reward. You are serving the Lord Christ. (Col. 3:23–24)

We should work heartily in Christ's service. But we leave the issue of "success" or worldly criteria of significance to him. If we are successful in a small way or in a huge way, we praise him for it. We rejoice in it. If as a result of our service we build a large organization or produce significant cultural achievements or put through sweeping political changes, we praise him. But we should guard our hearts, lest we contaminate our service by rejoicing in our own glory displayed in success, rather than in the glory of God. He has displayed *his glory* by working his success. And ultimately, our "success" will be the success of inheritance to be disclosed in the new heaven and the new earth. We cannot calculate that endpoint from within this life. "We walk by faith, not by sight" (2 Cor. 5:7).

15

Education

We have been following the themes in Kuyper's book on the lordship of Christ, *Lectures on Calvinism*. As mentioned earlier, the book's six chapters were compiled from six lectures that Kuyper was invited to give in 1898 at Princeton Seminary. If he had given seven lectures, we might possibly have enjoyed a chapter on the topic of education. Education had an important place in Kuyper's vision, as we can see from the energy and thought he put into the founding of the Free University of Amsterdam.[1] Kuyper also tried to educate the larger public through his popular writings in newspapers.

Education Honoring Lordship

If Christ is Lord of all of life, he is clearly Lord of education. All education should have the glory of God as its goal, the commandments of Christ as its norms, and the love of Christ as its fundamental motive. In addition, formal education has a key practical role in training young people for a life of serving

---

[1] "The Free University was at the heart of Kuyper's dreams. Here he could fulfill all his callings at once: scholar, institution-builder, leader, liberator, and guide of the common people" (James D. Bratt, ed., *Abraham Kuyper: A Centennial Reader* [Grand Rapids, MI: Eerdmans, 1998], 461).

Christ. What is taught in schools, how it is taught, and for what purposes it is taught all have a profound influence on the next generation.

The responsibility for training children in the way of the Lord comes out profoundly in the words in the Old Testament that form the context of the greatest commandment, the commandment to love God:

> Hear, O Israel: The LORD our God, the LORD is one. You shall love the LORD your God with all your heart and with all your soul and with all your might. And these words that I command you today shall be on your heart. You shall teach them diligently to *your children*, and shall *talk of them* when you sit in your house, and when you walk by the way, and when you lie down, and when you rise. You shall bind them as a sign on your hand, and they shall be as frontlets between your eyes. You shall write them on the doorposts of your house and on your gates. (Deut. 6:4–9)

A similar point is made in the book of Proverbs. Proverbs begins with an extensive section where a father instructs his son (chaps. 1–9). The text of Proverbs sets an example for all Israelite fathers and, by implication, also for mothers. It applies also to Christian parents and educators to this day. Both Deuteronomy and Proverbs discuss instruction or education that takes place primarily in the informal setting of family give-and-take. But the principles have implications when we come to consider settings for formal education in schools, colleges, and universities.

The theme of parental instruction in the Bible has connections with God's instructions to us, his children. God is like a father to Israel.

> My son, do not despise the LORD's *discipline*
>   or be weary of his reproof,
> for the LORD reproves him whom he loves,
>   as *a father the son* in whom he delights. (Prov. 3:11–12)

This Old Testament teaching has its climax in the New Testament. The New Testament declares that God is our Father through Jesus Christ the unique Son:

> But when the fullness of time had come, God sent forth his Son, born of woman, born under the law, to redeem those who were under the law, so that we might receive adoption as *sons*. And because you are sons, God has sent the Spirit of his Son into our hearts, crying, "Abba! Father!" So you are no longer a slave, but *a son*, and if a son, then an heir through God. (Gal. 4:4–7)

Because God is our heavenly Father, he undertakes to instruct us through discipline.

> And have you forgotten the exhortation that addresses you as *sons*?

> "My *son*, do not regard lightly the *discipline* of the Lord,
>   nor be weary when reproved by him.
> For the Lord *disciplines* the one he loves,
>   and *chastises* every *son* whom he receives."

It is for *discipline* that you have to endure. God is treating you as *sons*. For what *son* is there whom his *father* does not *discipline*? If you are left without *discipline*, in which all have participated, then you are illegitimate children and not *sons*. Besides this, we have had earthly *fathers* who *disciplined* us and we respected them. Shall we not much more be subject to the Father of spirits and live? For they *disciplined* us for a short time as it seemed best to them, but he *disciplines* us for our good, that we may share his holiness. For the moment all *discipline* seems painful rather than pleasant, but later it yields the peaceful fruit of righteousness to those who have been trained by it.

Therefore lift your drooping hands and strengthen your weak knees, and make straight paths for your feet, so that

what is lame may not be put out of joint but rather be healed.
(Heb. 12:5–13)

God's relation to us as our heavenly Father serves as a model for understanding the responsibilities involved in human education.

We also see the theme of spiritual instruction in Jesus's teaching. Jesus speaks of the value of his words as words instructing us in life:

> Everyone then who hears these *words of mine* and does them will be like a wise man who built his house on the rock. And the rain fell, and the floods came, and the winds blew and beat on that house, but it did not fall, because it had been founded on the rock. And everyone who hears these *words of mine* and does not do them will be like a foolish man who built his house on the sand. And the rain fell, and the floods came, and the winds blew and beat against that house, and it fell, and great was the fall of it. (Matt. 7:24–27)

The resources of biblical theology are relevant in studying this theme and can continue to enrich our understanding of the theological foundation and meaning of education. We have a great future of growing in knowledge, not because of our own power and wisdom, but because of the power and presence of the Lord (Matt. 28:20).

16

Work

Finally, let us consider the implications of the lordship of Christ for *work*.

The Nature of Work

In a sense we have been considering various kinds of work all along. "Work" in a broad sense includes not only whatever people are *paid* to do but all kinds of tasks. Since Christ is Lord of all, he is Lord over each and every task. He is Lord over details as well as general purposes. He is Lord over small tasks no less than big ones. The key verses in Colossians are relevant: "Whatever you do, *work heartily, as for the Lord* and not for men, knowing that from the Lord you will receive the inheritance as your reward. You are serving the Lord Christ" (Col. 3:23–24).

It is especially worthwhile to meditate on the scope of Christ's lordship because modern cultures often give us the message that only certain kinds of activity really matter. Many people suppose that jobs matter in proportion to how much pay someone receives for doing them. According to this way of thinking, having a million-dollar job in business or sports or entertainment matters. Being a grocery clerk or a waiter or a salesperson in a retail store does not matter much. Being a mother raising children does not matter at all, because you have no paycheck to show for it. Being a thoughtful neighbor exercising hospitality does not matter, because you are not paid.

But personal relationships do matter to the Lord. Each personal relationship is an opportunity to serve him by obeying the commandment to love your neighbor. And when we love our neighbor out of love for God, we are also loving God himself in the process.

Consider, in particular, the task of raising children. It is a weighty responsibility. Children are human beings made in the image of God. What a privilege and a challenge to guide them in growing to maturity! Will they learn to love God and love their neighbor? Or will they learn to follow the messages of culture that invite them to serve themselves by accumulating money and power? Will they learn to indulge in more and more avenues of pleasure for selfish purposes? How will parents guide them?

Parents have a challenging task in teaching and guiding their children (Eph. 6:4). We who are parents should be acknowledging our sins in this area and asking forgiveness through Christ. Parenting is not a way to earn our salvation but a labor of love to be undertaken because we are already saved and pardoned. We should be asking the Lord for wisdom and seeking to learn from the Bible's instruction.

The Offices of Prophet, King, and Priest

We may also consider work more deeply by studying the biblical-theological themes of the three offices of prophet, king, and priest. In the Old Testament, God appointed these special offices. We may call them offices because in many cases they were officially recognized. Everyone knew that Elijah and Elisha and Isaiah were prophets. Kings in Israel were officially anointed, as in the case of Saul in 1 Samuel 10:1 and David in 1 Samuel 16:12–13. The priests were officially consecrated in ceremonies like that in Leviticus 9–10. They were anointed in preparation for performing specific tasks.

What were the tasks? There were many. And in the Old Testament, there sometimes was overlap between the tasks and functions of the three offices. If I may simplify, the prophets communicated the word of God to the people. The kings ruled over the people whom God put under them. If they ruled well, they ruled by imitating and re-expressing God's rule and his standards of justice. The priests mediated the presence of God and the blessing of God to the people. They represented the people when they drew near to the special symbolic presence of God in the tabernacle and the temple of Solomon. And by offering sacrifices for the people, they mediated forgiveness of sins, which came from God to the people through the priests.

All of these offices are important because they foreshadowed three aspects of the work of Christ, the Messiah, who was still to come. Christ is the *final* Prophet, King, and Priest, who summed up, deepened, and brought to a climax what was symbolized in the Old Testament. Christ's fulfillment of the three offices is explained in the space of a few verses in Hebrews:

> Long ago, at many times and in many ways, God spoke to our fathers by the *prophets*, but in these last days he has *spoken* to us by his Son, whom he appointed the heir of all things, through whom also he *created the world*. He is the radiance of the glory of God and the exact imprint of his nature, and he *upholds the universe* by the word of his power. After *making purification* for sins, he sat down at the right hand of the Majesty on high. (Heb. 1:1–3)

Verses 1–2 compare Christ to the Old Testament prophets, through whom God spoke in former times (v. 1). Then the writer says, "In these last days he has *spoken* to us by his Son" (v. 2). Clearly the Son is like a prophet in bringing the word of God. But he is the supreme, final Prophet, because his message is climactic and he is himself God (v. 3).

Next, verse 3 describes Christ as upholding "the universe by the word of his power." A king in the Old Testament ruled over a limited territory. Christ is the universal ruler. He was also ruler at the time of creation "through whom also he [God] created the world" (v. 2). Thus, he is the supreme and final King.

Finally, he is the supreme and final Priest. Hebrews explains this aspect of Christ's work at greater length in later chapters (Heb. 2:10–3:6; 4:14–16; 7:1–10:39). But it mentions his priesthood briefly in 1:3 by referring to the fact that Christ made "purification for sins," which was the task of the priests.

The Westminster Shorter Catechism sums up the meaning of all three offices this way:

Q. 23. *What offices doth Christ execute as our Redeemer?*

A. Christ, as our Redeemer, executeth the offices of a prophet, of a priest, and of a king, both in his estate of humiliation and exaltation.

Q. 24. *How doth Christ execute the office of a prophet?*

A. Christ executeth the office of a prophet, in revealing to us, by his word and Spirit, the will of God for our salvation.

Q. 25. *How doth Christ execute the office of a priest?*

A. Christ executeth the office of a priest, in his once offering up of himself a sacrifice to satisfy divine justice, and reconcile us to God; and in making continual intercession for us.

Q. 26. *How doth Christ execute the office of a king?*

A. Christ executeth the office of a king, in subduing us to himself, in ruling and defending us, and in restraining and conquering all his and our enemies.

The Offices of Believers

Christ has fully provided for our salvation in every way. His work as Prophet, King, and Priest is perfect. All who believe in him are united to him and receive the benefits of his work. But it is also true that by being united to Christ, believers receive the power to function in some ways as imitators of Christ in their own tasks.

Consider, for example, the office of prophet. Christ speaks the final word of God in perfection. Our words are not perfect. But when we are filled with the Spirit of Christ, we can begin to bless others by speaking the word of Christ that we have learned from Scripture: "Let *the word of Christ* dwell in you richly, teaching and admonishing one another in all wisdom, singing psalms and hymns and spiritual songs, with thankfulness in your hearts to God" (Col. 3:16). So in a subordinate sense we become "prophets."

And in the last days it shall be, God declares,
that I will pour out my Spirit on all flesh,
and your sons and your daughters shall *prophesy*,
    and your young men shall see visions,
    and your old men shall dream dreams;
even on my male servants and female servants
    in those days I will pour out my Spirit, and they shall
      prophesy. (Acts 2:17–18)

How do we serve as kings? We serve as kings when we receive power from the Spirit of Christ and begin to rule righteously in areas over which God has given us responsibility. Thus, fathers and mothers are to rule wisely over their children in the family (Eph. 6:4). An employer is to rule in his business with the wisdom of Christ (Eph. 6:9).

How do we serve as priests? Christ has fully atoned for sins. We do not need to make any atonement. But we can approach God with confidence. Jesus has opened the way for us to approach God's presence in heaven, rather than merely the symbolic presence in the tabernacle on earth. The privilege that we have of approaching God exceeds what even the high priest in the Old Testament had.

Let us then with confidence *draw near* to the throne of grace,
that we may receive mercy and find grace to help in time of
need. (Heb. 4:16)

> Therefore, brothers, since we have confidence to enter the holy places by the blood of Jesus, by the new and living way that he opened for us through the curtain, that is, through his flesh, and since we have a great priest over the house of God, let us *draw near* with a true heart in full assurance of faith, with our hearts sprinkled clean from an evil conscience and our bodies washed with pure water. (Heb. 10:19–22)

We can approach God in prayer. And through our prayers, we may bring blessing to those for whom we pray. We may intercede for others. First Peter 2:5 confirms that we have been made priests: "You yourselves like living stones are being built up as a spiritual house, to be a *holy priesthood*, to offer spiritual sacrifices acceptable to God through Jesus Christ."

Applications to Work

We can use the categories of prophet, king, and priest in a metaphorically extended sense to see that many human activities involve service to God that imitates the "big" versions of these offices that appear in Scripture. For example, the office of prophet can be metaphorically extended to any form of communication and any form of handling of knowledge. All communication is related by analogy to the original communication by God in the Word of God. All human knowledge has divine knowledge as the original from which it derives.

The office of king can be extended to any form of rule or exercise of dominion. Rule over other human beings has a distinct character because human beings are made in the image of God. Some people, like parents and officers of civil government, have been appointed by God to have authority over others. But a ruler must not rule selfishly or tyrannically. He must respect the human beings for whom he is responsible and try to work for their good, rather than merely to increase his own power and wealth and prestige.

In other situations, God has given people responsibility over the subhuman creation. A farmer rules over his land, his crops, and his animals. A computer technician rules over computers by maintaining and repairing them. A dishwasher rules over the dishes by cleaning them. A woodworker rules over wood by shaping and crafting it. An electrical engineer rules over things electronic. In all these roles God empowers us to serve Christ by ruling in accordance with his standards.

How do we metaphorically extend the office of priest? I have talked about interceding for others before God. But all kinds of work that aim at human reconciliation and human blessing through personal relationships have a distant kinship with the office of priest.[1]

Many kinds of tasks involve combinations of prophetic, kingly, and priestly work. They simultaneously involve knowledge and communication (a prophetic aspect), exercise of power (a kingly aspect), and personal relationships where benefit can be passed from person to person (a priestly aspect). For example, parents in their relationship to children have complex, multidimensional interactions. They communicate. They make rules and enforce them. They guide their children toward maturity. They bless them with their gifts and also with their discipline. They pray for them. They teach them God's Word.

The analogies with the three offices of prophet, king, and priest are useful to us because they can help us to see the significance of work in God's sight. Work is not just a grind, not just a way of earning enough money to get by. If we have a prestigious job admired by the world, our work is still not mainly a way of getting honor and prestige. We serve the Lord Christ (Col. 3:24). And in serving him, we are also imitating him. We should be praying that through his Spirit we may receive power to serve with all our heart.

---

[1] See Vern S. Poythress, *Redeeming Sociology: A God-Centered Approach* (Wheaton, IL: Crossway, 2011), 202–4.

Part 4

TRAPS TO AVOID IN OUR SERVICE

17

Traps in Motivation

As we serve Christ, the resources of Scripture itself have a prime, irreplaceable role. Scripture alone is infallible instruction from God. But we have noted also that there is value in later resources that are based on Scripture. We may learn from Abraham Kuyper and his successors, from the Reformation, and from Augustine.[1] Kuyper's life now lies almost a hundred years in the past. The Reformation lies almost five hundred years behind us. And Augustine's strong emphasis on the sovereignty of God, which was one of the resources for the Reformation, lies even further back. With this much history behind us, we have plenty of resources. The past also gives us examples to imitate—and sometimes to avoid. There are failures as well as successes. And in some cases we can see the influence of sin.

So let us consider some of the traps into which people can fall, even when they are trying to honor the lordship of Christ. There are many traps. I cannot even list them all. But this and the next chapters can at least make a beginning.

---

[1] See Bruce Riley Ashford, *Every Square Inch: An Introduction to Cultural Engagement for Christians* (Bellingham, WA: Lexham, 2015), 46–64, for six short historical sketches.

Classification of Traps

For convenience, I will classify the traps into three main groups: traps in motivation, traps in judgments about norms, and traps in assessment of the situation. These three correspond to John Frame's three perspectives on ethics: the existential perspective (focusing on motivation), the normative perspective (focusing on norms), and the situational perspective (focusing on the situation).[2]

Frame's three perspectives overlap one another and reinforce one another. So our grouping into three categories includes corresponding overlaps. I will thus classify the traps according to which kind of focus is more prominent in any one trap. But all three perspectives are, in the end, relevant for each kind of trap. In addition, as an extra subdivision under the situational perspective, we will consider a fourth kind of trap—traps concerning hopes for the future.

In this chapter we consider traps that have to do with failures in motivation. These traps are most evident when we use the existential perspective.

PRIDE

The first trap is *pride*. Pride has been a fundamental human problem ever since the fall. From one perspective, it can be seen as lying at the root of every sin whatsoever. Whenever we sin, we are saying that our own judgment is superior to God's. That is pride. And we can see pride functioning when in Genesis 3 Adam and Eve listen to their own ideas (at the instigation of Satan).

Serving Christ as Lord means serving him above ourselves. It means crucifying our pride. Jesus calls on us to give up our own self-sufficiency, even our own *life*, for his sake:

> Then Jesus told his disciples, "If anyone would come after me, let him deny himself and take up his *cross* and follow me. For

[2] John M. Frame, *Perspectives on the Word of God: An Introduction to Christian Ethics* (Eugene, OR: Wipf & Stock, 1999).

whoever would save his life will lose it, but whoever *loses his life* for my sake will find it. For what will it profit a man if he gains the whole world and forfeits his life? Or what shall a man give in return for his soul?" (Matt. 16:24–26)

So, should we not expect that the people who are most devoted to serving Christ as Lord in all of life would be the most free from pride? Yes, we might expect that. But pride can creep in unawares. We can conceal from ourselves that we are taking pride even in our grasp of the principle of Christ's lordship. We begin to say to ourselves: "*We* understand and honor this principle of lordship, while these other, less zealous Christians do *not*. Look at how well we are doing!" In addition to pride focused on our intellectual grasp of principles, we can take pride in our energetic *practice* as we participate in Christian movements and endeavors to honor Christ in politics, or business, or education. We say to ourselves, "We are *doing* something, while so many lazy Christians are *not*."

Since pride is so insidious, it is worthwhile reflecting briefly on some of its dangers and how the Bible provides resources for overcoming pride. Exalting Christ means humbling ourselves and not overestimating our own importance, our own purity, or our own power.

> For by the grace given to me I say to everyone among you not to *think of himself more highly* than he ought to think, but to think with *sober judgment*, each according to the measure of faith that God has assigned. (Rom. 12:3)

> Put on then, as God's chosen ones, holy and beloved, compassionate hearts, kindness, *humility*, meekness, and patience. (Col. 3:12)

Through the universal rule of Christ, God rules over his kingdom. We do not. It is true that the Bible promises that we who belong to Christ are already seated in the place of authority with

Christ: "[God] made us alive together with Christ—by grace you have been saved—and raised us up with him and *seated us with him* in the heavenly places in Christ Jesus, so that in the coming ages he might show the immeasurable riches of his grace in kindness toward us in Christ Jesus" (Eph. 2:5–7). This position of authority is part of the heritage of every Christian believer even now (note the past tense, "seated"). It belongs to every Christian, not just those who have special understanding. But the authority is qualified: it is spiritual authority, wholly derivative from our union with Christ, and wholly subordinate to him.

"Building the Kingdom of God"

Some Christians like to think that they are "building the kingdom of God." But this kind of expression easily leads to equating our work with God's work. God is the King. Fundamentally, it is God who brings his kingdom.[3] The kingdom comes through the supernatural work of the Holy Spirit. The praise goes to God alone for his reign, as the Bible indicates:

> We give thanks to you, Lord God Almighty,
>   who is and who was,
> for you have taken your great power
>   and begun to *reign*. (Rev. 11:17)

> Hallelujah!
> For the Lord our God
>   the Almighty *reigns*. (Rev. 19:6)

Even within this age, God's kingly work of salvation takes place in the lives of Christians. In this connection, God is pleased

---

[3] One difficulty is that the expression *the kingdom of God* has a range of uses. We may speak of God ruling in providence over the whole universe (Ps. 103:19). Or we may focus on the *saving* rule of God, the work of God saving people in Christ (Col. 1:13). We may focus on the active *rule* of God or the *realm* over which his rule has sway. Rule and realm go together, and so do providence and salvation (Christ in his exaltation rules over all, Eph. 1:20–22; see chap. 2, "The Story of Redemption," above). We need to avoid artificial polarization. But we also need to make distinctions. Not everyone who lives under God's providence is saved. This whole book is meant to promote understanding of the lordship of Christ in a way that avoids the traps.

to use our humble service in the process of redemptive transformation. But it is necessary for it to be *humble* service, or else in practice we are acting in opposition to his kingdom rather than for it, however much we may claim the opposite. It is well worthwhile for us periodically to review the character of discipleship, as described by the Lord himself:

> But Jesus called them to him and said, "You know that the rulers of the Gentiles lord it over them, and their great ones exercise authority over them. It shall not be so among you. But whoever would be great among you must be *your servant*, and whoever would be first among you must be *your slave*, even as the Son of Man came not to be served but to *serve*, and to give his life as a ransom for many." (Matt. 20:25–28)

Rashness and Haste

Rashness can also be a trap. Our zeal can exceed our knowledge. Then we rush in to some project or some theory without adequate insight or maturity. We claim to be serving Christ, and we have an excitement about our service, but in haste we may fail to consider better routes, or wiser routes, or potential liabilities to the route that we have chosen. There is no easy solution to this trap. We can consult with others, who may see what we do not. We may also strive to grow in patience.

Despair

We can fall into the opposite problem from pride and rashness, namely, despair. We despair of accomplishing anything significant for the glory of Christ. We tell ourselves that the times are bad. Or we wallow in our past failures. But, paradoxically, this kind of reaction can conceal pride underneath. We are reacting as if we have no motivation unless we can do some great thing that will make us look great or transform the culture. If instead we learn humility, we will begin to serve the Lord joyfully without worrying about past failures or about whether we will see some glorious achievement by worldly standards.

Passive Piety

Passive piety is another trap. By *passive piety* I mean the view that it is always more pious to be passive and weak than to be active and strong. If we have this view, we may never arrive at a point where we are brave enough to start to serve the Lord in a new way or in a new direction. For some people, this passive piety can be a form of pride. They are afraid to make a mistake and be seen to fail.

Passive piety of this kind is a distortion. The Bible counsels us to serve, which is passive in one sense, and to be patient, which may involve a period of waiting rather than of activity. But it also counsels us to be active, as a number of passages confirm:

> Do you not know that in a race all the runners run, but only one receives the prize? So *run* that you may obtain it. Every *athlete* exercises self-control in all things. They do it to receive a perishable wreath, but we an imperishable. So I do not *run* aimlessly; I do not box as one beating the air. (1 Cor. 9:24–26)

> Therefore, my beloved brothers, be steadfast, immovable, always abounding in the *work* of the Lord, knowing that in the Lord *your labor* is not in vain. (1 Cor. 15:58; see also Phil. 2:12–13; 2 Tim. 2:6; 4:7)

Obedience to the Lord is what counts, not passivity or activity as a universal rule.

Timidity

Closely related to the trap of passive piety is timidity. We may fail to serve the Lord as we ought to because we are timid. We are afraid of failure or afraid of our own inadequacies. This kind of fear is the opposite of rashness. But if it overwhelms us, we will fail to serve the Lord with vigor. It is worthwhile remembering Paul's exhortation to Timothy:

> For this reason I remind you to *fan into flame* the gift of God, which is in you through the laying on of my hands, for God gave us a spirit not of fear but of *power* and love and self-control. Therefore do not be ashamed of the testimony about our Lord, nor of me his prisoner, but share in suffering for the gospel by the power of God. (2 Tim. 1:6–8)

FEAR OF MAN

Fear of man also interferes with serving Christ. The remedy is to fear God. It drives out the fear of man. If we are in fellowship with God, we will care what he thinks, and what he thinks outweighs all human opinion.

> But even if you should suffer for righteousness' sake, you will be blessed. Have *no fear of them*, nor be troubled, but in your hearts honor Christ the Lord as *holy*, always being prepared to make a defense to anyone who asks you for a reason for the hope that is in you; yet do it with gentleness and respect, having a good conscience, so that, when you are slandered, those who revile your good behavior in Christ may be put to shame. (1 Pet. 3:14–16; see also Isa. 8:11–13)

DEFENSIVENESS

Defensiveness may be one form of pride or fear or both. When we are criticized or attacked, our pride may be hurt or we may fear having our weaknesses exposed. We react with defensiveness. Instead, we should see whether we can learn from the criticism but then move on. We are serving the Lord, not human opinion—either good or bad. But it is also true that there are appropriate times to defend the honor of God. So we must be wise about what we choose to defend and how we do it.

Summary

All kinds of mixed motivations can corrupt service to Christ. These mixed motivations all stem from sinful inclinations of various kinds, some of which are subtle and difficult to uproot. We should remember that sanctification comes primarily from fellowship with Christ in the Spirit, not just from introspection.

18

Traps in Norms

Traps arise also when we follow improper norms for serving Christ. Norms that people hold can be either sound or distorted when compared with God's standards. Both explicit and implicit norms play a vital role in guiding Christian conduct and Christian service. So it is important to reckon with ways in which our norms can be corrupted or distorted.

Motivations (see the previous chapter) influence norms. Likewise, norms influence motivations. We cannot strictly separate the two. But for convenience we group together a number of traps that have a close tie with the issue of norms.

Heterodoxy

The first trap concerning norms is the trap of heterodoxy, that is, false doctrine masquerading as Christian truth. True doctrine contributes to spiritual health. False doctrine or heterodoxy destroys spiritual health. For some people, the word *doctrine* connotes stuffy, artificial discussion of irrelevant topics. But doctrine rightly conceived is a summary or re-expression of scriptural teaching. And God gives this teaching not only to make known the truth but also to guide us into spiritual health. We can see the way that truth leads to health when Jesus says, "Sanctify them in the truth; *your word* is truth" (John 17:17). When properly received, the truth is an instrument for sanctification, that is, for spiritual growth and health and holiness. Likewise, 2 Timothy 3:16–17 indicates how Scripture is profitable: "All Scripture is breathed out by God and *profitable* for teaching, for reproof, for correction, and for training in righteousness, that the man of God may be complete, equipped for every good work" (2 Tim. 3:16–17).

By contrast, false teaching destroys spiritual health. So it is no wonder that the New Testament writings repeatedly warn against it. For example, Paul warns against false teachers and indicates that they will try to corrupt the church: "I know that after my departure fierce wolves will come in among you, not sparing the flock; and from among your own selves will arise men speaking twisted things, to draw away the disciples after them" (Acts 20:29–30).

In our day, a gradual drift or a sudden jump into theological liberalism is one danger. Liberalism replaces the genuine gospel with a god of its own devising, which it supports by selectively chosen passages from the Bible. Liberalism is soul destroying. More visibly, it is church destroying. In the long run, people affected by liberalism leave the church for the world, and without the leaven of Christian faith, the culture becomes corrupted. Genuine Christians who are left find themselves discouraged and isolated, and often weakened.

Doctrinalism

A trap at the opposite pole from heterodoxy is doctrinalism. *Doctrinalism* is our label for the tendency for people to think that purity and precision in doctrine are the *only* things we really need to solve all our spiritual problems. According to this kind of thinking, doctrine *automatically* leads to changed lives. And changed lives among individuals automatically lead to changes in society—changes in worldview, in theory making, in education, and in social and political structures.

In fact, it is not that simple. We can find ourselves in a situation of "dead orthodoxy," where many church members can recite doctrine but do not display the practical *effects* of doctrine in holy living. Or we can find people whose lives are transformed on the level of individual morality and who display the fruit of the Spirit in individual behavior, but who do not have a sense of how their faith should make them think and act differently in science or art or politics.

Legalism

Another trap is legalism. *Legalism* describes any view that our good works are either a part or the whole of the *basis* for salvation. It says that we are saved by our works or by our goodness, while the Bible says that we are saved by the grace of God (Eph. 2:8–10). (There is also an *opposite* error, antinomianism, which has several forms. People may discount the importance of Christian obedience as one aspect of how we live in response to God's grace. Or they may depreciate the value of the divine commandments found in the Bible.)

Legalism in a subtler form includes a variety of views that make the law central to the whole process of salvation. One form would be to say that we are initially saved by grace, but then our continuation in a state of salvation depends wholly on our self-powered obedience to the law. Note that this view is *not* the same as the positive use of the law as a guide to Christian obedience. Christians ought to rely on Christ and on his Spirit to empower their obedience to commandments—to law: Jesus said, "If you love me, you will keep my *commandments*" (John 14:15).

Legalism can creep into Kuyperian circles and into the desire to serve Christ as Lord if we forget that it is Christ who, through his Holy Spirit, must empower us. Or we may produce a form of legalism if we add to or subtract from the commands of Christ in Scripture. The problem is real for people who have a desire to bring change in society. They may develop rules to guide their thinking, rules to guide social interactions, and rules to guide the construction of new social institutions. It is natural that people should look for rules of this kind to help them venture into more uncharted territory. But there is a danger that these rules come to be treated as *binding* on any Christian who wants to serve Christ.

The danger arose in a particular way with the neo-Kuyperian movement of cosmonomic philosophy. According to the view of Herman Dooyeweerd, details in biblical instruction became the responsibility of theology, which was sharply distinguished from philosophy and other specialized academic studies. In the hands of some followers of the cosmonomic philosophy, this move led to minimizing the role of biblical standards. And when biblical standards are minimized, they are replaced with something else. That something else could be either Dooyeweerd's cosmonomic philosophy itself or the so-called "norms" that belonged to each distinct modal sphere of the cosmos (aesthetic sphere, economic sphere, social sphere, historical sphere, and so on). These norms can begin to function like extrabiblical standards that govern people's lives.

The Bible indicates that God rules the whole cosmos. His rule is a "norm" in the sense that he controls what happens. But that is not the same as an ethical norm for human living. Scripture provides the ethical norms. God's providential control includes control over all human actions, good and evil. So we cannot use our observations of the situation around us to produce new norms for conduct, that is, norms that would add to Scripture rather than re-express scriptural commandments.

Externalism and Formalism

Closely related to legalism is the trap of externalism and formalism. For sinful human nature, it is always easier to try to obtain sanctity by following external rules than by cleansing the heart (which only God can do!). A movement to change society can easily fall into the trap of *just* trying to change society and no longer worrying about purity of heart or the glory of God.

Subjectivism

Subjectivism describes the trap of overconfidence in our feelings and intuitions in trying to serve Christ. In a sense, this can be seen as the opposite pole from externalism. Rather than overplaying rules and inventing extrabiblical rules, it underplays rules. In particular, it underplays the commands articulated in Scripture itself and the broader guidance that Scripture gives through the full textures of its instruction.

This danger arises as we try to work out the implications of the universal lordship of Christ, because working out the implications is not always easy or obvious. For some people, it is tempting to short-circuit the process by just relying on intuitions for what is proper service. But intuition, which is one focus of the existential perspective, needs to interact with reflection (expressing the normative perspective) and careful examination of the situation in society (expressing the situational perspective).

Philosophism

Philosophism is my label for the trap of depending too much on philosophy, even a philosophy that aspires to be distinctively Christian or Calvinistic. Philosophical reflection tends to produce high-level generalities about society and about the nature of the world, generalities that in the past have had only a distant relation to the instruction in Scripture. The service to Christ in all of life should anchor itself more firmly in Scripture.[1]

Loose Interpretation of Scripture

If Scripture is going to have a decided influence on our manner of serving Christ, it is important to interpret Scripture in a sound way. Whole books are devoted to discussing how to interpret the

---

[1] Vern S. Poythress, *Redeeming Philosophy: A God-Centered Approach to the Big Questions* (Wheaton, IL: Crossway, 2014), chap. 2; John M. Frame, *The Doctrine of the Knowledge of God* (Phillipsburg, NJ: Presbyterian and Reformed, 1987), 85–86; John M. Frame and Leonard Coppes, *The Amsterdam Philosophy: A Preliminary Critique* (Phillipsburg, NJ: Harmony, 1972).

Bible.[2] We need the help of the Holy Spirit as we study the Scripture. We need to proceed with the conviction that the Bible is indeed the very word of God. And we need love for Christ. We need to deepen our fellowship with the living God.

We may content ourselves at this point with drawing attention to traps found in two extremes. The first of these is a loose interpretation of Scripture. People may tell themselves that only the overall purpose of Scripture matters. They read for the general picture but gloss over details. When this takes place, there is much danger that in subtle ways they will end up conforming Scripture to their preconceived ideas or to prejudices in the larger cultural environment.

Wooden Interpretation of Scripture

The opposite danger is what we might call a wooden interpretation of Scripture. Some people have little sense for the literary artistry of Scripture, or its use of metaphor and poetic imagery, or the way in which Scripture uses ordinary language and ordinary means of communication rather than technical precision. Such people force an artificial precision upon Scripture and end up with conclusions that begin to make people as mechanical as the procedures they use. Conclusions of that kind often feed back into a kind of legalism. We can see the effect with the Jewish leaders of Jesus's time. Though they were experts in the details, they missed the central concern for knowing God. Accordingly, Jesus accused them:

> But Jesus answered them, "You are wrong, because you know neither the Scriptures nor the power of God." (Matt. 22:29)

> Woe to you, scribes and Pharisees, hypocrites! For you tithe mint and dill and cumin, and have neglected the weightier

---

[2] Vern S. Poythress, *God-Centered Biblical Interpretation* (Phillipsburg, NJ: P&R, 1999); Poythress, *Reading the Word of God in the Presence of God: A Handbook of Biblical Interpretation* (Wheaton, IL: Crossway, 2016).

matters of the law: justice and mercy and faithfulness. These you ought to have done, without neglecting the others. (Matt. 23:23)

There is no shortcut to growing in understanding Scripture and understanding the God who speaks in Scripture. Each aspect of understanding aids the other. It is important to grow because a deep understanding of Scripture is vital as we endeavor to serve Christ creatively in situations that the Bible does not address directly. The Bible as the word of God addresses everything either directly or by way of implication. It speaks to all of life. But it may take reflection and meditation to see how.

19

Traps in Situations

We now consider traps that have to do more with how we interact with the situations in our social environment.

Politicizing

One trap is to politicize the Christian faith. Politicization takes place if Christians think that the kingdom of God comes *primarily* through political change, or if they think of Christianity as a building block for the primary purpose of getting to an earthly political goal. Christians then invest their energy primarily in political involvement and in attempts to bring about political change by electing new officials and passing new laws.

We could say a good deal positively about the value of political involvement. As noted earlier, during much of his life, Abraham Kuyper was heavily involved in politics. A chapter of his book *Lectures on Calvinism* is devoted to the topic. Kuyper is right that Christ is Lord over the political sphere and over every politician and over every political decision. It is right that Christians should be encouraged to be involved in politics. As the Lord calls them, some Christians should seek to serve the Lord vocationally in offices of civil government. Being in government or politics is not intrinsically "dirty" or sub-Christian, as some of the Anabaptists have thought. The laws and practices of civil government make a difference for good or ill. They can serve the glory of God, or not. They can serve for genuine blessings for human beings, or not. It is important for people to work for laws that are in harmony with biblical ethical teaching.

On the other hand, political involvement brings with it temptations. Desire for power—even for good reasons—can be very corrupting within our fallen world. Though power can be used for good purposes, it is one of the biggest idols of our time.

The greatest and most impressive human concentration of power is found in civil government. Many people look for the government to solve their problems and expect it to do more than it will ever be able to do. The state becomes in their eyes a messianic substitute that will deliver us from war, strife, pollution, crime, hatred, racism, poverty—you name it.

It will deliver us, they think, if only the right people are in control. Precisely because people over-invest their hopes in government, Christians need to be a voice of caution. And many of us need to dial down our hopes for producing major cultural change through politics. Many other factors, such as family, education, news, and entertainment, influence cultural directions. Evangelism influences cultural directions as one person after another comes to Christ! Let us not forget that. At the same time, others among us need to be encouraged not to despair or give up completely on the political sphere, as if change were impossible, or Christian faith irrelevant, or politics too dirty, or God were not in control of the whole political sphere.

Movementism

Movementism is my ugly label for an ugly reality, the tendency of people to idolize a movement with which they are identified. And that tendency can catch us who are Christians. It can catch us even when the movement is supposedly defined as an endeavor to honor Christ as Lord in all of life.

Movementism is closely related to pride. We are proud to be part of a larger band of people. We tell ourselves that "we all" who are in the movement grasp the Kuyperian vision, while lesser Christians do not.

It is easy to identify our particular movement with the cause of Christ. Christ said, "Whoever is not with me is against me, and whoever does not gather with me scatters" (Luke 11:23). But he also said, "For the one who is not against you is for you" (Luke 9:50.) There is a subtle difference between these two statements. Christ's lordship implies that allegiance to him is not a matter of indifference. If you are not *with him* by following him, you are already rejecting him as Lord. And that means that you are *against him.*

But the same is *not* true of Christ's *disciples.* The disciple is a servant of the master. If we are disciples, we do not demand that people serve *us.* And we do not measure other people's allegiance to Christ by looking at whether they join *us.* So we must guard against the prideful tendency to exalt *our* movement and look down on anyone outside it.

Being Truly Reformed

With some shift in labels, the same lesson holds not only for a movement but also for a *theological position.* The Kuyperian movement to honor Christ as Lord of all of life has roots in the Reformed tradition. So those of us who are Reformed in our theology may take pride not in a "movement" but in our tradition. When we say to ourselves, "We are Reformed!" the implication can easily be that we are superior to those ill-informed Christians who are not. Actually, Reformed theology is supposed to be about exalting the grace of God and giving all the glory to him. What a horrible disgrace that it should be turned into its opposite—a source of pride and a basis for claiming superiority!

Unfortunately, it happens. Sin creeps in unnoticed.

Being Truly Kuyperian

We may not use the label *Reformed* to proclaim our superiority, but perhaps we use the label *Kuyperian* with pride. We tell ourselves that we are heirs of Abraham Kuyper and his marvelous vision and achievements. We can indeed praise God for raising up Abraham Kuyper. But let us also crucify our pride if it springs into action when we attach our names to his.

Withdrawal from the World

Withdrawal from the world and into Christian enclaves is another trap. The world has become too messy and too ungodly for us. So we cease interacting. We stop reaching out to those trapped in its meshes. We withdraw into our Christian subculture, where we can be comfortable and safe, and can receive reinforcement when we denounce the culture and mourn over our loss.

But actually we are not safe in any subculture, because sins creep in subtly, in the form of pride and superiority and selfish withdrawal. The only remedy is in repentance and in the joy of serving Christ from the heart. And that means loving our neighbor, including our neighbor who is immersed in a corrupt culture.

Assimilation to the World

The opposite trap from withdrawal is assimilation. This trap often becomes the deeper danger for intellectuals. And it is the deeper danger for many a young person who is homeschooled but curious about the music and entertainment in the world.

The Kuyperian vision tells us that serving Christ in all of life means working to express his lordship in all the arenas in which the non-Christian world meets us. So we affirm that we will interact with culture. And we do interact. If we are good at it, we interact from the standpoint of distinctively Christian commitments and a distinctively Christian worldview.

We interact, but without knowing it, we can also absorb assumptions and ways of thinking that have subtle corruptions. So we ourselves become corrupted little by little. It is easy to compromise rather than risk appearing obnoxious and fussy and dogmatic and inflexible by refusing to drift with the cultural flow. If we resist, people will tell us, "What a hypocrite you are; so unloving!" Moreover, it is easy to be fascinated by products or trends that seem brilliant or beautiful but are tainted with powerful cultural poison.

Downgrading the Institutional Church

It is tempting for modern-day Kuyperians to downgrade the institutional church, to underestimate its importance. Kuyperians may locate the center of action in cultural involvement. Going to church on Sunday becomes merely a time to "refuel" for that cultural activity. Kuyper himself saw that the institutional church was important. He was a major figure in the church split that resulted in part of the membership in the Dutch Reformed Church (*Nederlandse Hervormde Kerk*), a new denomination with solidified doctrinal commitments.[1]

It is worthwhile reminding ourselves that Jesus Christ founded the *church*, not a political party or a school (Matt. 16:18–19). Every believer in Jesus is united to Christ. And if he is united to Christ, he is also united to the body of Christ, the church. The members of the body of Christ depend on one another for their spiritual health (1 Corinthians 12). We do well to realize that the vigor and health of any cultural influences from Christians depend on the vigor and health of the church, which is chosen by God and empowered by him.

Moreover, by the power of God the church will survive even if the culture in which we live comes crashing to the ground. Jesus says, "I will build my church, and the gates of hell shall not prevail

---

[1] However, in his personal *practice* it appears that Kuyper was not an ideal model. James Bratt notes that he frequently missed attending church (James D. Bratt, *Abraham Kuyper: Modern Calvinist, Christian Democrat* [Grand Rapids, MI: Eerdmans, 2013], 129).

against it" (Matt. 16:18). He has no such promise for the culture of the United States or the culture of the Netherlands or other cultures where Christians live. Even if Christians have virtually no cultural influence, even if they are persecuted and imprisoned and killed as in North Korea and Saudi Arabia and Iran today, they are honored by God as part of the body of Christ.

Giving Importance Only to the Church

The opposite trap is to consider the institutional church the *only* significant organization of interest to Christians, to which they should devote their spiritual energy. According to this approach, what happens inside the walls of the church building is the only thing important to God, and thus the only thing that should be important to Christians. The rest of life is thought to flow almost automatically out of our church meetings, if only we run them with sufficient care and purity. A related temptation is to become focused too much on the external organization of the church and too little on spiritual reality.

We may call this kind of thinking *ecclesiasticism*. It is a trap that is parallel to doctrinalism. In both cases, the theory says that if we do one thing sufficiently well (church management or doctrine), we do not need to worry about anything else.

20

Traps concerning Future Hopes

Finally, we consider traps related to our hopes for the future. We are continuing the focus on the situational perspective, which began in the preceding chapter. Hopes for the future are a natural subtopic within a situational perspective.

The Relation of the Future to Our Situation

What happens in the future is not directly part of our *present* situation, but it forms a part of our situation in a broader sense. As time passes, it *will be* part of our situation or environment. And as we think about possibilities for the future, that will clearly have an influence on what we think we should do now to improve our situation.

At the same time, hopes for the future have a powerful influence on us because they offer a *motive* for action in the present. We are motivated when we think about how some cultural influence now might contribute to a glorious, healthy future. So the topic of future hope has a close connection with the *existential* perspective, which focuses on motivations. And, in addition, it has a close connection with the *normative* perspective, because the normative instruction in Scripture forms the most essential basis for informing us about what our hopes should be.

We might argue, then, that the topic of future hope involves all three of Frame's perspectives—situational, existential, and normative. And we could easily have linked it with any of the three preceding chapters about traps instead of dealing with it here.

Reliance on Postmillennialism

The first trap related to future hope is the trap of overrelying on postmillennialism. Postmillennialism is the view that Christ will come back and appear in his visible glory only *after* a long period during which the Christian faith prospers and the cultures of the world are transformed under Christian influence. According to this view, in the future the number of Christians will multiply until Christianity is the dominant religion worldwide. Christians will grow in maturity so that their activities in the world are more consistently sanctified. As a result, Christian faith will function as a "leaven" in the cultures of the world, and a grand era of peace, prosperity, and godly living will begin. This long period is customarily called "the millennium." Postmillennialism is one of three major millennial views. The other two are amillennialism and premillennialism.

Some positive biblical emphases belong to each of the three millennial positions. Consider amillennialism, which was Abraham Kuyper's position.[1] According to this view, Christ may come back at any time to bring in the new heaven and the new earth (Rev. 21:1). If there are many years yet until he comes, we may hope that the Christian faith prospers. The gospel "is the power of God for salvation to everyone who believes" (Rom. 1:16). Jesus has commissioned us to "make disciples of all nations" (Matt. 28:19). But amillennialism does not find a firm biblical basis for believing that there *must* be a long period of prosperity before Christ returns.

---

[1] Amillennialism is also my preferred position; but there is no need to argue the matter here. See Vern S. Poythress, "2 Thessalonians 1 Supports Amillennialism," *Journal of the Evangelical Theological Society* 37, no. 4 (1995): 529–38, accessed May 11, 2015, http://www.frame-poythress.org/2-thessalonians-1-supports-amillennialism/.

A considerable number of passages in the Old Testament talk about the glories of the coming kingdom of God. But these passages are fulfilled in the first and second comings of Christ. The second coming is the biggest and grandest fulfillment of all. The promise of these two stages of fulfillment makes it questionable whether the Old Testament passages *require* still another phase of fulfillment, a time of distinct millennial prosperity. (This distinct stage is what is postulated by both premillennialism and postmillennialism.)

Now, what about the trap? The trap does not lie in postmillennialism itself. It lies in making the postmillennial view a main *motivation* for serving Christ in all of life. The argument may appeal to Old Testament prophecies that tell of the coming reign of Christ and his glory. These prophecies, it is thought, should be a main motivation for serving Christ. We serve him because our service contributes to moving history toward the goal of millennial prosperity and the display of the glory of Christ on earth.

There is much to respect in this kind of reasoning. Certainly we *should* be motivated to seek the glory of Christ. And we should long for the day when his glory is displayed in its full extent and magnificence, as it will be in the new heaven and the new earth: "And I saw no temple in the city, for its temple is the Lord God the Almighty and the Lamb. And the city has no need of sun or moon to shine on it, for *the glory of God* gives it light, and its lamp is the Lamb" (Rev. 21:22–23). We should rejoice as we see Christ's glory displayed in our own day, as people become a "new creation" (2 Cor. 5:17) and are transformed into the image of Christ and display his glory in their lives (2 Cor. 3:18).

But note that the full display of the glory of God and of the Lamb comes in the new heaven and the new earth, not in a millennium. The New Testament encourages believers to hope for the return of Christ (Acts 1:11; 1 Cor. 16:22), not for a millennial prosperity detached from or prior to his second coming. We need to have our motivations right and our hopes rightly directed.

Here are some potential ways in which our hopes might deviate from scriptural teaching:

1. *Depending on the guarantee of worldly success.* Should we serve Christ only because we are guaranteed successful fruit in the form of a coming millennial prosperity? No. We serve him because we love him and because we are committed to obeying his commandments. We will bear fruit far more than we can imagine in the new heaven and the new earth.

2. *Setting our hopes on a coming millennium.* Postmillennialists believe that Christ cannot come *except* on the other side of the time line that runs through the long period of time of earthly prosperity called the millennium. As we have indicated, they may be right. Postmillennialism is a respected interpretation of the Bible. But it is not the only alternative. In practice, it is easy for postmillennialists to fix their hopes primarily on the near goal, the goal of the millennium, rather than the far goal, the goal of the second coming. This choice of the millennium as the *primary* goal is in tension with the New Testament, which teaches believers to fix their hopes on the coming of Christ (1 Corinthians 15; 1 Thess. 4:13–5:11; 2 Thessalonians 1; Titus 2:13; 1 Pet. 1:13; 2 Pet. 3:8–13; Rev. 22:20).

3. *Using a (possibly) false hope.* The continuing discussions over the question of the millennium show that postmillennialism is not clearly established by Scripture. It is unwise to build a large-scale foundation on a hope that the Bible does not clearly endorse. We *do* hope for the second coming of Christ and for the new heaven and the new earth. That hope is firmly established because it is clearly taught in Scripture. If God had wanted the millennial hope to function in a central way in Christian motivation, he could have written the New Testament in a way that gave it a more central, prominent role. We must be guided not only by what we think is true but by the actual organization of the Bible, which gives indications about what is more important.

4. *Investing in our kingdom building.* In discussing the trap of

pride, we reflected on the perils of picturing our service to Christ as a way of "building the kingdom of God." The idea that we are laying the first bricks in a structure of millennial prosperity easily plays into human pride. And it easily tempts us to a kind of exclusivism, where *our* kingdom is identified with the kingdom of God.

Relying on Carryover into the New Heaven and the New Earth

Another hope among some Christians is the hope that the products of cultural labors within this world will carry over into the new heaven and the new earth. This hope is different from postmillennialism because it focuses not on a future millennium but on God's promise of the consummation, that is, the new heaven and the new earth of Revelation 21:1–22:5. Nevertheless, it is similar to postmillennialism in another way, in that it provides a motivation for present-day cultural involvement by linking that involvement to future fruit or future success. The fruit comes to maturity not in the millennium but in the consummation.

We need to consider carefully this theory of carryover to avoid a potential trap. First, this view is healthy in stressing that the created world in which we live, though corrupted by sin, is still fundamentally a *good* creation. Caring for this world that God made is a way of serving and honoring God. Appreciating the blessings that God gives us in this world is a positive way of honoring God. We must avoid the temptation of *asceticism* and *world denial*, which despises creation. The Bible pointedly criticizes such asceticism:

> Now the Spirit expressly says that in later times some will depart from the faith by devoting themselves to deceitful spirits and teachings of demons, through the insincerity of liars whose consciences are seared, who forbid *marriage* and require abstinence from *foods* that *God created* to be received with thanksgiving by those who believe and know the truth. For *everything created by God* is good, and *nothing is to be*

rejected if it is received with thanksgiving, for it is made holy by the word of God and prayer. (1 Tim. 4:1–5)

But the theory of carryover says something more. It says that the good things in this world will carry over into the next world, the world of the consummation. It cites in its favor two passages in particular:

For the creation waits with eager longing for the revealing of the sons of God. For the creation was subjected to futility, not willingly, but because of him who subjected it, in hope that the *creation itself* will be *set free* from its bondage to corruption and obtain the *freedom* of the glory of the children of God. (Rom. 8:19–21)

By its light [the light of the new Jerusalem] will the nations walk, and the kings of the earth will bring *their glory* into it, and its gates will never be shut by day—and there will be no night there. They will bring into it *the glory and the honor of the nations*. (Rev. 21:24–26)

The first passage, from Romans 8, draws an analogy between creation and the sons of God. The sons of God will receive a future revelation in glory in their resurrection bodies. The point to notice is that the sons of God are transformed in their bodies but still maintain continuity with their present bodies. In a similar manner, the creation as a whole is to be "set free" (Rom. 8:21), which means that it will not be annihilated but transfigured. We might say that, figuratively speaking, the creation as a whole will undergo a kind of "death and resurrection," analogous to the death and resurrection of Christ and the death and resurrection of Christian believers. There is a kind of destruction in death. But life on the other side of physical death exists, in resurrected bodies. And these bodies are a transfiguration or renewal of the old bodies, not a completely new start.

We know that there is substantial continuity between the resurrection bodies of the saints and their present bodies, because their resurrection follows the pattern of Christ's resurrection.

> But our citizenship is in heaven, and from it we await a Savior, the Lord Jesus Christ, who will *transform our lowly body* to be like *his glorious body*, by the power that enables him even to subject all things to himself. (Phil. 3:20–21)

> Just as we have borne the image of the man of dust, we shall also bear the *image* of the *man of heaven* [Christ]. (1 Cor. 15:49)

In his resurrection body, Christ still had the nail prints in his hands (John 20:25). The disciples were able to recognize him. By analogy, we may infer that the new heaven and new earth will be a recognizable transfiguration of the present heaven and earth.

The obvious objection to this theory of carryover is that the present heaven and earth will be burnt up.

> But the day of the Lord will come like a thief, and then the heavens will pass away with a roar, and the heavenly bodies will be *burned up and dissolved*, and the earth and the works that are done on it will be exposed. Since all these things are thus to be dissolved, what sort of people ought you to be in lives of holiness and godliness, waiting for and hastening the coming of the day of God, because of which the heavens will be *set on fire and dissolved*, and the heavenly bodies will melt as they *burn*! But according to his promise we are waiting for *new heavens and a new earth* in which righteousness dwells. (2 Pet. 3:10–13)

Bible interpreters disagree about the details of the transition to the new heaven and new earth. Some interpreters stress the language of dissolution in 2 Peter 3. They maintain that the new heaven and the new earth will be virtually a fresh start. There will be almost *no continuity* with the present heaven and earth. This view recognizes that there has to be some minimal continuity, because those who have believed in Christ will enter this new world. They will basically be the *same* people, though with transformed bodies, like the resurrection body of Christ. But, according to this way of thinking, that is about all we can expect. The creation itself, as distinct from the human beings within it, will be totally destroyed.

In reply, the advocates of continuity can point again to Romans 8:19–21. Verse 21 says that the creation will be "set free." It is not annihilated. Moreover, 2 Peter 3, with its passage about dissolution, need not be interpreted as implying total annihilation. In verses 5–7 of the same chapter, 2 Peter compares the earlier destruction by the water of Noah's flood to the coming destruction by fire. "The world that then existed was deluged with water and *perished*" (v. 6). But the new world after Noah's flood was very like the old one in many ways. It had human beings; it had the same kinds of animals; it had the same physical earth and the same heavenly bodies as before. Moreover, the language of fire in 2 Peter 3:10–12 can be understood as fire of *purification*, not fire of *annihilation*. The main effect is that the new heaven and new earth are places "in which *righteousness* dwells" (v. 13). In a parallel manner, Noah's flood destroyed human wickedness, not the creation as such.

In sum, 2 Peter 3:10–12 implies purification, not complete annihilation. So it is compatible with the teaching about the transfiguration found in Romans 8:19–21. We can still affirm continuity between the present heaven and earth and the consummation.

The language of "new heavens and new earth," which sounds to many people so radical, goes back to Isaiah 65:17. The subsequent verses, Isaiah 65:18–25, describe the new heaven and the new earth in some detail. It sounds remarkably like a transfigured world, with many points of continuity with the present one.

EVALUATING THE THEORY OF CARRYOVER

So what should we think about the relation of the present heaven and earth to the new heaven and earth? We can affirm a considerable measure of continuity between the present heavens and earth and the future. Romans 8:19–21 is important. And the example that we get with Christ's resurrection body is important, showing us that transfiguration does not undercut a measure of continuity.[2]

But the theory of carryover involves something more. It suggests that what will carry over is not only saved human beings and their transfigured bodies, not only a transfigured heaven and earth, but *cultural products*. Will Leonardo da Vinci's *Mona Lisa* be in the new heaven and the new earth? Will J. S. Bach's cantatas and organ pieces be there? If a Christian businessman builds an effective factory for manufacturing, will the factory be there? Some of the advocates of carryover cite Revelation 21:24–26, which talks about the kings of the earth bringing into the new Jerusalem "the glory and the honor of the nations." Does that include the *Mona Lisa* and other cultural products?

The picture in Revelation involves the nations bringing tribute to honor God and the Lamb, who is the great King of the world. In Revelation 21 we have a wonderful imagistic description. John describes the new world in images that use analogies from the present world. But they are analogies rather than identities. They are imagistic rather than photographic. God has surprises for us. So we cannot calculate beforehand exactly what the new world will be like in detail.

Christ in his resurrection body had memories of what he had said (Luke 24:44) and what Peter had said and done (John 21:15–17). By analogy, it looks as though in our future life we will remember this life. We will remember how much grace God showed to us in forgiving our sins. If that is the case, it is possible that some people may also remember the *Mona Lisa* and Bach's music. And if musicians remember music, could they not also construct instruments and perform the music? It seems logical. But the Bible does not go into such details.

---

[2] John Murray, *Redemption Accomplished and Applied* (Grand Rapids, MI: Eerdmans, 1955), 178–80; Cornelis P. Venema, *The Promise of the Future* (Carlisle, PA: Banner of Truth, 2000), 456–68.

So we need to be cautious lest we build on false hopes. Yes, there is continuity. But there is also transfiguration. The Bible says that "the present form of this world is passing away" (1 Cor. 7:31). It tells us not to invest hopes in this world as if everything will continue into the next world just as it was before.

God's "Carryover"

More important than any of our memories is God's memory. God knows all things, past, present, and future. His knowledge is comprehensive and perfect. In particular, God knows forever all the details of the *Mona Lisa* and Bach's cantatas and the Christian businessman's factory. Not only that, it was he who empowered and sustained the creativity of the artists and the businessman! If God wishes, he may create as part of his new earth a new *Mona Lisa* or new scripts of Bach's cantatas or a new factory. Or he may create a *transfigured* form of these things that belonged to the old world. Or not. *It is up to God.*

God may choose to reward Leonardo da Vinci or J. S. Bach or others who served him in this world by creations that God brings about in the new world. In the end it was God who created Bach's cantatas, through the gifts and talents and experience and energy that he gave to Bach. All the glory belongs to God. Bach himself acknowledged this very principle by signing his works *SDG*, initials standing for the Latin expression *soli deo gloria*, "to the glory of God alone."[3] God, not Bach, receives the glory both in this world and in the world to come.

So there is no difficulty with imagining that God might recreate Bach's cantatas in the new world. *It is up to him.* It should be enough for us to let God be God, and to acknowledge his infinite wisdom. What he does is far better than what we can conceive, using just our plans or our imaginations (Eph. 3:20).

In the rewards from God there will be surprises. The kingdom

---

[3] Calvin R. Stapert, "To the Glory of God Alone," *Christian History* 95 (2007), accessed September 20, 2014, http://www.christianitytoday.com/ch/2007/issue95/1.8.html.

of God is a kingdom of grace and a kingdom of surprising reversals. "The last will be first, and the first last" (Matt. 20:16; see Mark 10:31; Luke 13:30). The widow who put in two small copper coins "put in more than all of them" (Luke 21:3). Only God can bring a perfect world with perfect answers for the struggles and sacrifices of this life.

TRUSTING RATHER THAN CALCULATING

In considering this issue, we need to bear in mind principles similar to what we have discussed for postmillennialism. The Bible does not dwell on issues relating to the *details* of the continuities and discontinuities between this world and the next. It does not spend a lot of space providing detailed hopes about carrying over some piece of this world into the next. It does not tell us what will happen to the *Mona Lisa*. It does not try to motivate us to serve the Lord now by saying that good-quality cultural products will last.

Instead, the Bible tells us to serve the Lord now because he is the Lord. He is worthy of our service. He sees our service. He remembers it (1 Cor. 15:58; Heb. 6:10). He remembers it perfectly. And he has a reward to give us (Col. 3:24). Those are solid promises. As for the details, the judgment is the Lord's, not ours.

> This is how one should regard us, as *servants of Christ* and stewards of the mysteries of God. Moreover, it is required of stewards that they be found *faithful*. But with me it is a very small thing that I should be judged by you or by any human court. In fact, I do not even judge myself. I am not aware of anything against myself, but I am not thereby acquitted. It is *the Lord who judges me*. Therefore do not pronounce judgment before the time, before the Lord comes, who will bring to light the things now hidden in darkness and will disclose the purposes of the heart. Then each one will receive his commendation *from God*. (1 Cor. 4:1–5)

We may be tempted to want some specific guarantee about the *Mona Lisa*—or whatever is our favorite cultural product. But behind that temptation is the idolatrous idea that our plans are better than God's, or our speculations are better than his promises. Instead, if we desire God himself, if we recognize him as the only God, we will get all our desire. When we are reconciled to God through Christ, we can have confidence that God loves us and cares for us. Even within this life, God has provided so much that is beautiful and delightful. We will experience complete joy in God when we enter the new world that he will make.

Triumphalism

A closely related trap is the trap of *triumphalism*. Triumphalism is more a collective mood than a specific doctrine. It is an atmosphere generated in a movement whose participants see their movement as the first wave in a series of achievements leading to progress, recognition, and cultural dominance. People are so confident that they feel they have already triumphed in principle. Even if they have a long road ahead of them with many formidable obstacles, their cause gives them a clear path to their goal, and the righteousness and efficacy of their cause assure them that they will attain the result. This trap of triumphalism is closely related to what I have called *movementism*.

Avoiding the Traps

Looking at the history of Christian movements can be like looking at a pattern of two steps forward, one step backward. We can find valuable achievements, and at the same time and in the same place we find sins and failures and misjudgments. And how shall we assess and sort through the combination of good and bad? We need solid standards and discernment to do it right. And we ourselves are part of the problem, because we ourselves still suffer from distorting views contaminated by sin. Such is the nature of human existence in this age. Two steps forward, one step backward.

We should learn from the traps at least two things. First, we must keep our eyes on Christ, not on how well we are doing. Second, we must learn humility. It is fitting to cite again some of the passages that I mentioned in chapter 17 in the discussion of pride:

> For by the grace given to me I say to everyone among you not to *think of himself more highly* than he ought to think, but to think with *sober judgment*, each according to the measure of faith that God has assigned. (Rom. 12:3)

> Put on then, as God's chosen ones, holy and beloved, compassionate hearts, kindness, *humility*, meekness, and patience. (Col. 3:12)

> For everyone who exalts himself will be humbled, and he who humbles himself will be exalted. (Luke 14:11)

Conclusion

What shall we conclude? Christ is our glorious Savior and Lord, who is worthy of all our allegiance. He has saved us and given us the sure guarantee of "an inheritance that is imperishable, undefiled, and unfading, kept in heaven for you" (1 Pet. 1:4).

He has forgiven our sins and given us perfect righteousness, the righteousness of justification by faith, because his perfection becomes ours when we are united to him by faith. He has also transformed us through the work of the Holy Spirit, so that we can begin to serve him faithfully within this world. He has given us a sure hope for his return and for the coming of the new heaven and the new earth (Rev. 21:1).

Christ is worthy of all the commitment and all the effort that we can give. He has given himself up for us all (John 10:17–18; Titus 2:14). How should we not give him our all? When we do so, we will have the joy that he has promised, even if in the midst of tribulation: "I have said these things to you, that in me you may have *peace*. In the world you will have *tribulation*. But take heart; I have *overcome* the world" (John 16:33).

In these ways, our prospects are bright, and our motivations are deep and powerful. Christ is Lord of all of our life, all the time. He works in us to transform all of our lives. As we change, our labors become more effective in bringing every area of life into the service of Christ.

But there are also powerful opponents. Satan himself is the

chief opponent of God. He opposes also those who belong to God and endeavor to serve him (Eph. 6:10–20). We can expect also to meet opposition from unbelievers and opposition from sins that still remain in us. The list of "traps" given in the previous section is a good reminder of the extent of the opposition, and a reminder that some of that opposition is subtle and difficult to uproot.

We must not be discouraged by any of this. We would be totally in despair if our work depended on our own perfection or our own power. But it does not. Awareness of opposition should always encourage us to return to Christ and to his promises and his power. Even imperfect work done in service to him will be rewarded.

If this book has encouraged you to commit yourself to Christ as Lord and to endeavor to serve him with all your heart, it has achieved its purpose. "Now to him who is able to keep you from stumbling and to present you blameless before the presence of his glory with great joy, to the only God, our Savior, through Jesus Christ our Lord, be glory, majesty, dominion, and authority, before all time and now and forever. Amen" (Jude 24–25).

Appendix

Two Kingdoms Theology

In our day a spectrum of views are classified under the term *two kingdoms theology*. Does this theology conflict with the view that Christ is Lord of all of life, as I have set it forth in this book? It may depend to some extent on which version of two kingdom theology we are looking at. Even a single individual can develop or modify or clarify his position over time. So it is a complex and challenging task to examine the whole field of positions that go under this label.

I will not undertake a thorough interaction and analysis here.[1]

[1] The literature is extensive. Listed here are only a few of the prominent sources supporting forms of two kingdoms theology or criticizing it: D. G. Hart, *A Secular Faith: Why Christianity Favors the Separation of Church and State* (Chicago: Dee, 2006); David VanDrunen, *A Biblical Case for Natural Law* (Grand Rapids, MI: Acton Institute, 2006); VanDrunen, *Living in God's Two Kingdoms: A Biblical Vision for Christianity and Culture* (Wheaton, IL: Crossway, 2010); VanDrunen, *Natural Law and the Two Kingdoms: A Study in the Development of Reformed Social Thought* (Grand Rapids, MI: Eerdmans, 2010); VanDrunen, *Divine Covenants and Moral Order: A Biblical Theology of Natural Law* (Grand Rapids, MI: Eerdmans, 2014); Michael Horton, *The Gospel Commission: Recovering God's Strategy for Making Disciples* (Grand Rapids, MI: Baker, 2011); Cornelis P. Venema, "One Kingdom or Two? An Evaluation of the 'Two Kingdoms' Doctrine as an Alternative to Neo-Calvinism," *Mid-America Journal of Theology* 23 (2012): 77–129; Venema, "Christ's Kingship in All of Life: Butchers, Bakers, and Candlestick-Makers in the Service of Christ," *Mid-America Journal of Theology* 25 (2014): 1–27; Ryan C. McIlhenny, ed., *Kingdoms Apart: Engaging the Two Kingdoms Perspective* (Phillipsburg, NJ: P&R, 2012); William D. Dennison, "Review of VanDrunen's *Natural Law and the Two Kingdoms*," *Westminster Theological Journal* 75, no. 2 (2013): 349–70; John Frame, "Review of David VanDrunen's *A Biblical Case for Natural Law*," accessed September 29, 2014, http://www.frame-poythress.org/review-of-david-van-drunens-a-biblical-case-for-natural-law/; and aspects of Frame, *The Doctrine of the Christian*

Rather, I want to continue to set forth a positive approach to understanding the lordship of Christ over all of life. I will do so by examining several kinds of distinctions that some forms of two kingdoms theology discuss and that are important in reflecting on the task of serving Christ. The way we understand the distinctions affects how we understand the lordship of Christ and its bearing on our lives.

Augustine's City of God and the Earthly City

In Augustine's book *The City of God* he makes an important distinction between what he calls "the city of God" (the "heavenly city") and the earthly city. The city of God is composed of those who love God. The earthly city is composed of those in rebellion against him.[2] Clearly, this is a distinction taught in Scripture and affirmed in Abraham Kuyper's and Cornelius Van Til's principle of *antithesis*. It is not an issue dividing them from the folk who talk about two kingdoms.

But this principial antithesis must not be confused with other distinctions that Augustine makes later in *The City of God*. For example, he says that the earthly city will no longer be a city when the final judgment is executed.[3] In this context, he is contrasting what is temporary within this age and what endures into the new heaven and new earth. He also discusses the use of earthly goods, which are created things and thus not part of the human and angelic polarization between the righteous and the wicked.[4] Augustine talks about civil government, which is an institution rather than a company of saved or rebellious individuals.[5] These later distinctions must not be conflated with the earlier antithesis between two kinds of human persons and two kinds of angels.

Life (Phillipsburg, NJ: P&R, 2008); Marcus Mininger, "Eschatology and Protology, Christ and Culture: Marriage as a Biblical Test-Case," *Mid-America Journal of Theology* 25 (2014): 117–40.
[2] Augustine, *The City of God*, in *A Select Library of the Nicene and Post-Nicene Fathers of the Christian Church*, ed. Philip Schaff, vol. 2 (Grand Rapids, MI: Eerdmans, 1979), 11.1.
[3] Ibid., 15.4.
[4] Ibid., 19.17.
[5] E.g., ibid., 18.21–22; 19.16.

Babylon and the Bride

The book of Revelation provides another important contrast for our instruction: the contrast between Babylon and the bride. The bride is the true people of God. Her purity is represented by her being clothed with "fine linen, bright and pure" (Rev. 19:8). By contrast, Babylon the prostitute is the morally corrupt, counterfeit bride. The contrast is fundamentally between true and false worship.

In the turmoil of the present age, we as human observers cannot always easily identify true allegiances of human hearts. In practice, people's actions are compromised. The book of Revelation often deals in black-and-white colors and absolute contrasts so that we can come to see the fundamental issues at stake. In the figures of the bride and the prostitute we have just such a depiction of fundamental issues. Do you serve God through Christ, and so lead a life of ethical purity, or do you serve sex and money and pleasure and the false gods of this world, and so lead a life of immorality?

The exact details about the interpretation of Babylon depend on a person's view of major interpretive issues in the book of Revelation. Does Babylon stand for the corruption of ancient Rome, or a general principle of moral corruption, or a final manifestation of wickedness shortly before the second coming? Even if it has reference to a specific time in history, the principle it embodies is more general.[6] And so Revelation contains lessons for us all.

Believers in Christ are part of the bride, the true church. Unbelievers, by contrast, ultimately participate in Babylon. The pictures of Babylon and the bride have pertinence both to the end of this age and to those living at any time within this age. We see the bride described in her glory in Revelation 19:7–8, in the context of the marriage supper of the Lamb (v. 9). This picture describes the celebration after Christ's second coming. At this point, the bride has been made perfect. But even while we are in this life,

---

[6] Vern S. Poythress, "Counterfeiting in the Book of Revelation as a Perspective on non-Christian Culture," *Journal of the Evangelical Theological Society* 40, no. 3 (1997): 411–18, accessed December 4, 2014, http://www.frame-poythress.org/counterfeiting-in-the-book-of-revelation-as-a-perspective-on-non-christian-culture/.

the church is the bride of Christ, according to Ephesians 5:25–26. The picture in Revelation 19:7–8 mentions "the righteous deeds of the saints," a reference to deeds they have carried out in this life. Similarly, Babylon symbolizes life within this age practiced in rebellion against God.[7]

This contrast between the bride and Babylon is thus similar to Augustine's contrast between the heavenly city and the earthly city. The bride stands for the true church, while Babylon stands for the false church. We should flee Babylon rather than mix with her, as Revelation indicates:[8]

Then I heard another voice from heaven saying,

"*Come out of her*, my people,
  lest you *take part in her sins*,
lest you share in her plagues;
for *her sins* are heaped high as heaven,
  and God has remembered *her iniquities*."
    (Rev. 18:4–5)

For all nations have drunk
  the wine of the passion of *her sexual immorality*.
    (Rev. 18:3; cf. v. 23)

This condemnation on Babylon confirms that it is a symbol for those who engage in false worship and immoral behavior instead of worshiping and serving the living God.

Babylon in Revelation should not be confused with the his-

---

[7] For further discussion, see, e.g., Vern S. Poythress, *The Returning King: A Guide to the Book of Revelation* (Phillipsburg, NJ: P&R, 2000), 159–72; G. K. Beale, *The Book of Revelation: A Commentary on the Greek Text* (Grand Rapids, MI: Eerdmans, 1999), 847–925.

[8] David VanDrunen counsels Christians to *participate* actively in the Babylon of Revelation 18: "It is important to note that *Christians* presently participate in the cultural activities of Babylon" (VanDrunen, *Living in God's Two Kingdoms*, 69, italics his; see also 91, 97). On the surface, this statement seems to contradict my view. But I am not sure how big a difference is found here. VanDrunen appears to me to interpret the Babylon in Revelation as similar to the historical Babylon of Daniel's day. He says at one point, "Revelation 18 refers to *this present world*, teeming with *cultural activities*, as 'Babylon'" (74, italics mine). By contrast, I think Babylon in Revelation is a symbol for false worship. In and of itself, that difference is minor. But it might lead, through further reasoning, to differences in how people construe the nature of Christians' involvement with surrounding cultures. And differences in this area might become major.

torical Babylon in which Daniel lived. The historical Babylon of Nebuchadnezzar's time offered a mixed culture and a mixed situation, containing both good and bad. Daniel and his three friends participated in the culture of Babylon in a general way. But they also met pressures and temptations to compromise and to practice idolatry. The situation in Daniel's Babylon has a general lesson for Christians in all times and places. It is always true that Christians are tempted to compromise with ungodly elements of culture. It is also true that Christians can participate in culture in ways that do not compromise their exclusive allegiance to Christ.

The imagery for Babylon in Revelation draws on Jeremiah and other Old Testament passages about historical Babylon. But a reuse of imagery does not imply identity in referent. If we collapse the two Babylons into one, it may open the door to confusion later on. In fact, this is a general problem in interpreting the book of Revelation. We must not confuse the moral and religious contrast between the city of God and the earthly city (akin to the bride and the prostitute of Revelation) with other contrasts, particularly the contrast between the church and culture.

Babylon is condemned and judged in Revelation 17–18. But is she condemned merely because she symbolizes society and culture or because she is wicked? If we identify Babylon in Revelation with the societies of this world, it could lead to unwarranted consequences. We could end up condemning all cultural activity as wicked (since Babylon is the prostitute, a picture of wickedness) or condoning Christian moral compromises (because we have no choice but to live in Babylon). These routes need to be avoided. And they can be more clearly avoided if readers understand that Babylon in Revelation is a symbol of worldly wickedness, not a symbol of culture or society in general.

Church and State

Another kind of distinction is the distinction between church and state. This distinction has been recognized for centuries, even within medieval Roman Catholic theology and practice. We can also find something analogous in the Mosaic era of the Old Testament. The law of Moses distinguishes judges, kings, prophets, and priests. It sets out distinctive roles and responsibilities for judges and kings, who are responsible for public justice (Ex. 18:13–27; Deut. 16:18–20; 17:14–20); they are thus analogous to modern officers of the state. The priests and Levites are responsible to care for holy things and to instruct people in God's law (Lev. 6:8; 21–22; Numbers 3–4; 8; Neh. 8:1–8; Mal. 2:6–9); they are thus analogous to the church.

But the analogies with the Old Testament are indeed analogies rather than identities, because Israel as a whole people was the people of God, a holy nation, distinct from all other nations (Ex. 19:5–6). Its distinctive character as a holy nation was a shadow and foretaste of the holiness of Christ and the holiness of his church.

Christ is now our Great High Priest. He has made obsolete the Aaronic priesthood of the Old Testament (Heb. 7–10). Christians have direct access to God through his mediation, not the mediation of earthly priests (Heb. 10:19–22). Thus, it is a mistake to think of New Testament pastors as priestly mediators for an unqualified laity. The laity themselves are now all priests (1 Pet. 2:5; Rev. 1:6; 5:10) through the great high priesthood of Christ.

> You yourselves like living stones are being built up as a spiritual house, to be *a holy priesthood*, to offer spiritual sacrifices acceptable to God *through Jesus Christ*. (1 Pet. 2:5)

> To him who loves us and has freed us from our sins by his blood and *made us* a kingdom, *priests* to his God and Father, to him be glory and dominion forever and ever. Amen. (Rev. 1:5–6)

> And you [Christ the Lamb of God] have *made them* a kingdom and *priests* to our God, and they shall reign on the earth. (Rev. 5:10)

In the end, everything depends on just how one understands the distinction between church and state. There are many views. They involve, among other things, how one understands the distinctive, limited powers that God has delegated to the authorities who are officers in the church versus officers in the state.[9]

ERRORS TO AVOID WITH CHURCH AND STATE ISSUES

Appalling consequences have ensued when the state has interfered with the affairs of the church, and vice versa. The most notorious evil consists in the persecution of people judged to be heretics. In late-medieval times, judgments of heresies were sometimes in the hands of state authorities, or in the hands of church commissions (the inquisition), or both. If the heretics did not recant, the state imposed on them bodily punishment (including death). In our day, severe abuses of power occur in some modern Islamic states. Governments suppress Christian worship and evangelism, and forbid people who are classified as Muslims from professing faith in Christ.

Such measures for allegedly protecting true religion are not only disastrous in practice but unjust. But to reach this conclusion, we must reflect on the power and the limits of the state, as revealed in Scripture.[10] God alone has ultimate authority to specify what falls within the state's responsibilities.

European history has seen its share of appalling consequences of state interference with the church. In many cases, officers of the state or nobles or patrons have had the privilege of appointing people to ecclesiastical office. And that practice has corrupted the church.

Whether state interferes with church or church with state, the people involved may claim they are serving Christ. But they are

---

[9] Vern S. Poythress, *Redeeming Sociology: A God-Centered Approach* (Wheaton, IL: Crossway, 2009), chap. 25.
[10] Vern S. Poythress, *The Shadow of Christ in the Law of Moses* (repr., Phillipsburg, NJ: P&R, 1995), part 2, "Understanding Specific Penalties of the Law."

mistaken. And the appalling consequences bring disgrace on the name of Christ.

It is also important to note the limited authority that God has given to the elders of the church. The elders are the officers appointed to rule over the church on behalf of Christ, the great Shepherd. They have a God-given responsibility to "shepherd the flock of God that is among you, exercising oversight" (1 Pet. 5:2). But they have authority only to call on the sheep to believe and do what Scripture teaches. It is not their responsibility to give pronouncements that go beyond the teaching of Scripture.

Scripture criticizes people who in the name of religion add extra rules for people to follow, supposedly for their religious benefit:

And he said to them, "Well did Isaiah prophesy of you hypocrites, as it is written,

"'This people honors me with their lips,
  but their heart is far from me;
in vain do they worship me,
  teaching as doctrines the commandments of men.'

You leave the commandment of God and hold to *the tradition of men.*" And he said to them, "You have a fine way of rejecting the commandment of God in order to establish *your tradition!*" (Mark 7:6–9)

If with Christ you died to the elemental spirits of the world, why, as if you were still alive in the world, do you submit to *regulations*—"Do not handle, Do not taste, Do not touch" (referring to things that all perish as they are used)—according to *human precepts and teachings*? These have indeed an appearance of wisdom in promoting self-made religion and asceticism and severity to the body, but they are of *no value* in stopping the indulgence of the flesh. (Col. 2:20–23)

People in the church, and especially officers in the church, need to take these warnings to heart. We must beware of adding to Scripture "human precepts and teachings" (Col. 2:22) that claim to bring spiritual advantages. In reality, they are "of no value" (v. 23).

These are steps that we must avoid. But we must also pay attention to what are the positive roles of church officers. The apostle Paul defines the task of the church positively in his discussion with the elders of the Ephesian church:

. . . to *testify to the gospel* of the grace of God. (Acts 20:24)

I did not shrink from declaring to you *the whole counsel of God*. (Acts 20:27)

The church has the task of declaring the gospel and, more broadly, communicating the Scripture, which is summed up in the expression "the whole counsel of God." It also has the responsibility of discipling its members and disciplining any who fall into sin (1 Corinthians 5).

In our day, as mentioned under the trap of "politicizing" (see chap. 19, above), the officers of the church can be tempted to make all kinds of pronouncements about political affairs—not just pronouncements about moral principles that are clearly taught in Scripture, but "meddling" pronouncements beyond the competence and authority of the church officers. Christian citizens may serve the Lord by voting or by being involved in political organizations or by being appointed as officers in civil government. But such service is not part of the responsibility of elders in their function *as elders* of the church.

We also need to remember that other institutions exist alongside the church and the state. Church and state are not the only authority structures that God has established. There are many spheres of human interaction. In addition to churches, there are institutions of *false* religion, such as temples, mosques, and "churches" that are churches only in name. There are economic institutions, educational institutions, and institutions for sports.

To be sure, historically the church and state and their relations with one another have proved to be the source of many tensions and fights. It is not hard to see why. People who are fond of the state are tempted to claim for the state unbounded and unlimited authority over everything else.

And people who belong to the church must proclaim the universal rule of Christ. Because of his rule, the state is responsible to obey Christ, and to submit to his standards of justice. The state is not a god on earth. Christ is the ultimate Lord, not Caesar. Conflicts will decrease only to the extent that both church and state submit to the rule of Christ the Lord and both reckon seriously with the *limited* authority that God has given to each kind of officer.

That said, it is still important to remind ourselves of the *many* institutions to which God has given responsibilities of various kinds. If we think only in terms of two—church and state—we unwittingly create a situation in which the state is tempted to take over as much as it can, gradually dominating more and more over every other institution *except* the church. And then it is all too easy for it to take the final step and crush the church, because the state has already come to regard itself as god on earth in every other way.

Special Grace and Common Grace

Another useful distinction is the distinction between special grace and common grace, a distinction introduced earlier (chap. 5). "Grace" is undeserved favor from God. *Special grace* is that specific kind of favor from God in which he brings salvation to his chosen people. Those who belong to Christ receive this special grace, the undeserved favor of salvation itself and all the benefits of salvation. Those without a saving relationship to Christ receive no special grace.

As long as people walk this earth, the gospel invitation comes to them. The gospel invites them, yes, *commands* them (Acts 17:30) to repent. They must come to Christ and be saved. If they turn to Christ, in that very act they are the recipients of saving grace, that is, special grace. But as long as they are outside of Christ, they receive only common grace.

Common grace describes those benefits of God that come to unbelievers as well as believers. Among these benefits are sun and rain (Matt. 5:45) and fruitful seasons providing food (Acts 14:17). These benefits are undeserved, so they are a form of grace. But they do not result in salvation. They are "common" because God gives them to both believers and unbelievers.

Believers receive common grace in the sense that they receive many benefits that externally look the same as the benefits that come to unbelievers. They receive sunshine and rain. But believers give God thanks for them (1 Tim. 4:4). They recognize that these things are personal gifts from a personal God. God expresses his care for each individual; he does not merely give gifts to a faceless multitude. Since God loves each believer with an everlasting love in Christ (Jer. 31:3), the benefits that come to believers are an expression of his special love to each of them. Thus, in a deeper sense, even these gifts that seem to be common are a matter of *special* grace when we see how they are rooted in God's personal love. They look the same "outside" as the benefits to unbelievers; but "inside," for those who understand God's revelation of his love to them, they are *not* the same.

The idea that God expresses his special, personal love for believers even in seemingly ordinary gifts is confirmed by several passages. In the Lord's Prayer Jesus teaches us to pray for ordinary benefits: "Give us this day our daily bread" (Matt. 6:11). We seek the benefit of daily bread through our personal relationship to God the Father in prayer. We do not merely assume that God will give bread to humanity as a nameless whole.

Jesus also promises that if we seek God's kingdom, all God's other benefits follow:

> Therefore do not be anxious, saying, "What shall we *eat?*" or "What shall we *drink?*" or "What shall we *wear?*" For the

Gentiles seek after *all these things,* and your heavenly Father knows that you need them all. But seek first the kingdom of God and his righteousness, and *all these things will be added to you.* Therefore do not be anxious about tomorrow, for tomorrow will be anxious for itself. Sufficient for the day is its own trouble. (Matt. 6:31–34)

First Timothy 4:4–5 indicates not only that we should give thanks for ordinary benefits but also that they are "made holy by the word of God and prayer": "For everything created by God is good, and nothing is to be rejected if it is received with thanksgiving, for it is *made holy by the word of God and prayer.*" The preceding verse (4:3) mentions marriage and food. Unbelievers marry, and unbelievers receive food. These two benefits, marriage and food, come from common grace when they come to unbelievers. But they have an additional meaning for believers. They are "made holy." That is, they are no longer "common" in the sense of being outside the holy sphere. They are God's holy gifts to holy people, namely, believers. The believers know the truth from the Word of God, and they pray, asking for these gifts and thanking God for them. Through receiving the Word of God and participating in prayer, believers in Christ have intimate fellowship with God in his holiness. They are holy people themselves. So believers receive these gifts of marriage and food as holy gifts.[11] The gifts then have a status of holiness, a status in which they are special gifts that flow from Christ to people in saving fellowship with God the Creator.

I have been talking about common grace and special grace, and the gifts that God gives to various human beings. What if we try to use the word *kingdom* in connection with these gifts? Is there, in some sense, a "kingdom" of special grace? There is—the kingdom of those who believe in Christ and thus are the members of the true church. And is there also a "kingdom" of common

---

[11] See also the reflections on marriage in Mininger, "Eschatology and Protology."

grace, the area on which God distributes common grace? The Bible does not use this specific terminology. In a sense the scope of common grace includes the whole world. But in another sense, common grace goes only to unbelievers. When *believers* receive from God something that looks "common" in an external way, it nevertheless has the status of being a holy gift, as we have seen. So in this sense, the "kingdom" of common grace would be the same as Augustine's earthly city. It is the company of those in rebellion against God.

God's Providential Rule and Christ's Saving Rule

We can also distinguish between the providential rule of God over all things and the saving rule of Christ over his people, who make up the church. This distinction is closely related to the distinction between common grace and special grace. Distinguishing these two kinds of rule is important in order that we appreciate the *special* care that Christ has for his people and the way in which they are distinct from the rest of the world in his eyes.

Within Reformed tradition, some people have said that as *God* Christ rules in providence together with the Father and the Holy Spirit; as *man* and as Messiah, he rules in bringing salvation to his church. And this may sound as if there are two separate ruling agents. But, of course, Christ is one person, God and man. We saw in chapter 2 that Christ's rule over all involves both his divine and his human nature. The idea that providence involves only Christ's divine nature is contradicted by the biblical passages that teach a *universal* authority *based* on Christ's victory. It is worthwhile to remind ourselves of some of these passages:

> And Jesus came and said to them, "*All authority* in heaven and on earth *has been given* to me. Go therefore and make disciples of all nations." (Matt. 28:18–19)

> Being therefore *exalted at the right hand* of God, and having received from the Father the promise of the Holy Spirit, he has

poured out this that you yourselves are seeing and hearing. For David did not ascend into the heavens, but he himself says,

> "The Lord said to my Lord,
> *Sit at my right hand*,
>   until I make your enemies your footstool."
>   (Acts 2:33–35)

. . . according to the working of his great might that he worked in Christ when he raised him from the dead and *seated him at his right hand* in the heavenly places, far above all rule and authority and power and dominion, and above every name that is named, not only in this age but also in the one to come. And he put *all things under his feet* and gave him as head over all things to the church, which is his body, the fullness of him who fills all in all. (Eph. 1:19–23)

He is the radiance of the glory of God and the exact imprint of his nature, and he upholds *the universe* by the word of his power. After making purification for sins, he *sat down* at the right hand of the Majesty on high, having become as much superior to angels as the name he has inherited is more excellent than theirs. (Heb. 1:3–4)[12]

The Ephesians passage is especially significant. It begins with a reference to the resurrection of Christ, thus linking the rest of the passage with what happened to Christ in his human nature. The resurrection was a vindication for his obedience, not merely a revelation of his deity. It is a climactic aspect of his work of salvation. It leads to being "seated" at the right hand of God. And Christ has "all things under his feet," according to Ephesians 1:22. This expression is quoted from Psalm 8:6, which talks about human beings having dominion.

Thus, the rule of Christ over "all rule and authority and power and dominion" is a rule that he exercises as the God-man, not

---

[12] See also 1 Cor. 15:25–26; Col. 1:18.

merely as God. He exercises this rule on behalf of the church, as the last part of Ephesians 1:22 indicates: "as head over all things *to the church*." Thus, his universal rule is closely related to his purposes for the church.

The church is distinct from the world; but Christ's rule over all things is a single, unified rule by the God-man. It is his one rule over "all things." At the same time, his unified rule is something that God has given "to the church" for her benefit. In accordance with this rule of Christ, "for those who love God *all things* work together for good, for those who are called according to his purpose" (Rom. 8:28). In this sense there is only *one* kingly rule, the rule of Christ.[13]

The Covenant with Noah and the New Covenant

We can also distinguish between two covenants: the "common grace" covenant with Noah in Genesis 8:20–9:17 and the covenant of grace that God makes with saved people throughout the generations.[14] In the New Testament period, the covenant of grace takes the form of the "new covenant" (Matt. 26:28; 1 Cor. 11:25; 2 Cor. 3:6–18; Heb. 8:6–13).

The human participants in the two covenants are distinct. The covenant with Noah extends to all Noah's descendants (Gen. 9:9) and even to the animals (v. 10). Thus, it includes unbelievers as well as believers. The new covenant, by contrast, extends only to believers. It is the covenant in which God promises salvation through union with Christ and his blood.

The distinction between these two covenants is important in

---

[13] Simon G. de Graaf makes the same point eloquently in "Christ and the Magistrate," trans. Nelson D. Kloosterman, in *Kingdoms Apart: Engaging the Two Kingdoms Perspective*, ed. Ryan C. McIlhenny (Phillipsburg, NJ: P&R, 2012), 95–109. He appeals to 1 Tim. 2:1–7, arguing that Christians pray for "kings and all who are in high positions" in order that they might be saved and their practice of ruling might be transformed as they submit to Christ. Likewise, he points to Ps. 2:8–11, which implies that the kings of the world should submit to God's Messiah. The same is implied by the expressions "the ruler of kings on earth" (Rev. 1:5) and "King of kings and Lord of lords" (Rev. 19:16; cf. 17:14) (see ibid., 96–99).

[14] The distinction between the two covenants plays a significant role in VanDrunen, *Living in God's Two Kingdoms*. For a defense of the distinct character of the postdiluvian covenant with Noah, see VanDrunen, *Divine Covenants and Moral Order*, 97–114.

order to preserve the nature of the church. The church is the body of Christ, whose members are those who have a saving relation to Christ. They are united to him by faith. Unsaved people have no part in the body of Christ.[15] We must resist the urge, seen in Europe even after the Reformation, to unite the whole populace through a common religious bond by making everyone within a single territory a member of the state-sponsored church. Geography does not create faith. And civil government does not create faith.

The two covenants, the common grace covenant with Noah and the new covenant, have two distinct circles of human beings who are objects of the covenant. The common grace covenant with Noah applies to all human beings, while the covenant of grace, in the form of the new covenant, applies only to Christians.

But there is complexity in the way the two covenants function in relation to one another. The gospel proclamation goes out to all, not merely to those who are already saved. God "*commands* all people everywhere to repent" (Acts 17:30). The gospel is ethically and religiously *binding* as a commandment to all, even though not all people respond by repenting. Moreover, Paul is a "minister" of the new covenant (2 Cor. 3:6), and his ministry is to proclaim the gospel (2 Cor. 4:4–6). The gospel announces the message of the new covenant. So *one aspect* of the new covenant, namely, the command to repent, includes unbelievers.

If unbelievers are morally obliged to repent, that is only the first step or the opening of a door into a lifetime of repentance. They are obliged to humble themselves, to come to Christ, and to serve him. Unbelievers are, of course, obliged not to murder or to commit adultery or to steal. They are obligated to the moral law,

---

[15] I am leaving in the background at this point the distinction between those who are *actually* saved, as known by God, and those who are members of the visible church (by baptism as an outward sign). "The Lord knows those who are his" (2 Tim. 2:19). But we do not. Nor do we know who may be a regularly attending church member and yet not actually saved. We only come to know that a person is an unbeliever if such a person apostatizes (as in 1 John 2:19). Until a person apostatizes, he belongs in an outward way to the community of grace, and this kind of "belonging" explains language like Heb. 6:4–8.

because God's standards of morality are universal. But they are *also* obligated through God's command in Acts 17:30 to repent and to serve Christ. Through that commandment, the entire new covenant is in fact pertinent to them. It is pertinent not because they are already heirs of salvation but because the covenant commands them to *become* heirs.

We may put it another way. Christ rules over *all*, and that includes those who are currently unbelievers. They are obligated to submit to him even though they do not *admit* their obligation. And since they should submit, they should obey *all* his commandments and *all* his teaching. His declarations are the commandments of the universal King, with the binding authority of the King.

(As other parts of this appendix make clear, the instructions and commandments of Christ, and more broadly the instructions of Scripture, include distinctions between believers and unbelievers, and between the church and other institutions. The universal authority of Christ gives us these distinctions and maintains them, rather than undermining them.)

The present rule of Christ is a central reality of our time. The covenant with Noah, though still relevant for the whole human race, only indirectly addresses this reality. It belongs to an earlier, incomplete stage in revelation. So it has decided limitations. It does not provide us with a direct indication of the full moral obligations of either Christians or non-Christians. The rule of Christ does. He has *all authority* (Matt. 28:18).

Natural Law and Scriptural Teaching

Another distinction that is sometimes made is between natural law and scriptural teaching. *Natural law* is a designation for the universal moral law of God, which binds all human beings, and which all human beings know through conscience.[16] Romans 1:32 indicates the existence of universal moral law: "Though they *know*

---

[16] The expression *natural law* is also used in other ways; but these need not concern us.

God's righteous decree that those who practice such things deserve to die, they not only do them but give approval to those who practice them." In addition, by indicting other nations around Israel, Amos shows that they are guilty for having violated God's moral standards (Amos 1:3–2:3).

On the basis of these and other verses, we know that the natural law does exist. And its existence is important. It means that human beings cannot escape God as Creator, nor can they escape his moral claims on them and their responsibility to him. They are guilty for having violated God's moral principles. Moreover, God's principles are not merely far off; human beings already know these principles. And in their hearts, at the deepest level of who they are as creatures, they cannot help but acknowledge these moral standards to be true and right. They cannot escape their guilt. Their hearts testify against them.

The existence of natural law also means that God's positive verbal revelation *in Scripture* does not come to people in a vacuum. It resonates with great power with what human beings already are as creatures in the image of God. God's moral pronouncements, as set forth in the Ten Commandments,[17] do not come as "arbitrary" impositions on some kind of human nature that is quite alien to them. Rather, they proclaim and reinforce and make specific what people already know about God at a deep level.

Nevertheless, there are three difficulties with natural law as a source for moral standards. First, the corruption of the human mind by sin leads to moral darkness. Pagans suppress and distort moral standards, and may sear their conscience.

> Now this I say and testify in the Lord, that you must no longer walk as the Gentiles do, in the futility of their *minds*. They are *darkened* in their understanding, alienated from the life

---

[17] The Ten Commandments have elements that are tailored to the redemptive-historical situation in which they were given. God had just redeemed his people Israel out of Egypt (Ex. 20:2); he met with them at Mount Sinai (19:18; 20:1, 19–21); and he gave instruction that included reference to the special Land of Promise (20:12). In addition to such special features, the Ten Commandments give expression to God's character and the moral laws that bind all human beings everywhere.

of God because of the ignorance that is in them, due to their hardness of heart. They have become callous and have given themselves up to sensuality, greedy to practice every kind of impurity. But that is not the way you learned Christ! (Eph. 4:17–20)

Now the Spirit expressly says that in later times some will depart from the faith by devoting themselves to deceitful spirits and teachings of demons, through the insincerity of liars whose consciences are *seared*. (1 Tim. 4:1–2)

Second, historically the expression *natural law* has been used in more than one context. Sometimes authors have reckoned with the corruption of the human mind—but sometimes not. In Roman Catholic contexts, it was sometimes assumed that human reason, though weakened, was essentially unfallen and able in principle to discern properly the nature of moral standards. Deists had even more confidence in reason than did Roman Catholics. For deists, *natural law* meant what reason could discern *independently* of Scripture. According to such approaches, scriptural law supplies essentially the same content as natural law, but by different means.

But such approaches have a flawed view—an overly optimistic and rosy view—of the power of unaided reason after the fall. And they have a flawed view of the role that God designed for the special revelation in Scripture. God designed from the beginning that we as human beings should be instructed and guided by his verbal communication to us, not merely by conscience. In addition, God provides regeneration and the indwelling of the Holy Spirit so that we may faithfully receive what he communicates. To encourage conscience and reason to function independently of Scripture, even for a while, is to oppose God's way.

Third, nothing in Scripture suggests that revelation of God through nature and through the constitution of mankind gives us more accurate, more detailed, or distinctive moral principles, differing from what we can find by a careful study of Scripture.

Quite the opposite—it is Scripture that has far more detail. Moreover, because Scripture gives us verbal communication, it is more difficult to evade and to distort than are the promptings of conscience.

The Role of Natural Law in Communicating with Unbelievers

It is sometimes suggested that, as a matter of strategy, we should appeal only to natural law when talking to non-Christians about moral issues, while we may appeal in addition to Scripture when we are talking to Christians. This strategy is recommended because many non-Christians do not recognize the authority of Scripture, and an appeal to Scripture gets nowhere in an argument.

A lot here depends on the details concerning what is actually being proposed. Are we talking about a temporary tactic that we use in *some* situations or about a long-range, permanent, exclusive strategy?

The whole universe testifies to God and to who he is (Ps. 19:1–2; Rom. 1:18–23). In discussions with a non-Christian, we can start anywhere because all facts are ordained by God. In this sense, conscience or a sense of right and wrong can be the starting point. Human nature itself, as a creation of God, testifies to its Creator. And in some cases an argument with this starting point might be persuasive. If it is effective, we have helped the other person see something true, and that is a good result.

But we could also choose to bring Scripture in right away. There is nothing wrong with revealing that you are a Christian believer and that you believe that the Bible has wisdom about moral and political questions. An unbeliever may respond with a scoff. But then that response provides an opportunity to engage the unbeliever, not about the narrow moral question with which you started, but about a far more central and important question, the question of who God is and what difference he makes.

In public political discussions, of course, there may be little opportunity for an extended interchange. But even here, we must reckon with the fact that the Bible really is the word of God, whether unbelievers acknowledge it or not. It really does have divine authority. By its divine authority it may persuade people even though they verbally deny that it is divine.

In the present Western environment, many people are becoming actively hostile not just to the Bible but to any mention of religious authority in the context of political or ethical discussion. That hostility is a sin problem and a cultural problem. Though the problem is with the culture, not with the Bible, it should nevertheless encourage us to exercise extra care in thinking about short-range tactics. For example, given the Western atmosphere, hearers may *misinterpret* an appeal to the Bible as something relevant only for Christians. Or they may think we are trying to "impose" a narrow churchly standard on all of society, as if we could not distinguish the people of God in the church from the rest of the citizenry.[18] This misinterpretation is compounded by the fact that a history of state churches in Europe has introduced confusion about how the Bible addresses humanity outside the church. In the light of such confusion, we want to make it clear that God is God of the whole universe and of all mankind. Christ is Lord of the universe, not just the church. God's moral standards apply universally.

The problems of misunderstanding are serious and call for care in communication. Yet these problems do not at all change the nature of moral authority or moral standards. The Bible is still the word of God. Its moral standards still have universal relevance (when properly understood).

For us, part of the challenge is to break through the rebellious spirit that refuses to listen to God. The Bible is freely available in Western cultures. And people know that it exists. But most people do not pay attention to it. By ignoring the Bible, they

---

[18] I am grateful to David VanDrunen for pointing out this problem to me.

show in practice that they despise the word of God. In despising God's word, they also despise God himself. That represents deep spiritual rebellion. If that rebellious spirit does not change in the culture at large, we are going to see many bad political decisions and many bad laws, however eloquent we think our arguments are when based on an appeal to conscience. If the conscience of the culture is rotten, it is as if you have a big hole in the bottom of the cultural "boat." However fast you bail out water using short-range appeals to conscience, more water will rush in. You will wear yourself out, and the boat will sink.

Why not stop panicking and talk soberly to the people in the boat about what they do not want to consider, the hole in the boat? They do not want to consider it because the only genuine way to repair the hole of moral rottenness is to turn to Christ for salvation. In comparison, short-range political arguments are not as important as we think. And, *by itself*, an appeal to natural law is not effective at all in turning people to Christ.

The Holy and the Profane

Next we have the distinction between the holy and the profane (the common). In the Old Testament, the tabernacle of Moses was holy after it had been ceremonially consecrated (Exodus 40). So was the temple that Solomon built (1 Kings 8). So were the Aaronic priests. By contrast, the space *outside* the tabernacle courtyard was called "common," in that it was open to all the people of Israel. But it was "common" only in a relative sense. The entire camp of Israelite people facing an enemy was holy (Deut. 23:14).

What does all this have to do with us? In the Old Testament, the holiness of the tabernacle and of the people of Israel functioned as a *type* or *shadow*, prefiguring the holiness of Christ and the holiness of the church as the body of Christ. Ever since the day of Pentecost, the church composed of Jew and Gentile has been the holy people of God. One of the distinctions between the church and the world is that the church is holy.

Do you not know that you are God's temple and that God's Spirit dwells in you? If anyone destroys God's temple, God will destroy him. For God's temple is *holy*, and you are that temple. (1 Cor. 3:16–17)

You yourselves like living stones are being built up as a *spiritual house*, to be a *holy priesthood*, to offer spiritual sacrifices acceptable to God through Jesus Christ. (1 Pet. 2:5)

Individual Christians are also holy, because the body of each individual is a temple of the Holy Spirit: "Or do you not know that your body is a *temple* of the Holy Spirit within you, whom you have from God?" (1 Cor. 6:19). Thus, Christians are called "saints," which means "holy ones," as illustrated in 1 Corinthians 1:2: "To the church of God that is in Corinth, to those *sanctified* [holy] in Christ Jesus, called to be *saints* [holy ones] together with all those who in every place call upon the name of our Lord Jesus Christ, both their Lord and ours."

If the church as a whole and all Christians as individuals are holy, what are the implications? The special holiness of the church and of individual Christians implies some special obligations.

In the Old Testament God gave distinct directions concerning the treatment of holy spaces, holy foods (the priests' food from sacrifices), and holy people. In God's instruction given through Moses, the people of Israel are declared to be "a kingdom of *priests* and a *holy* nation" (Ex. 19:6). The people as a whole are holy, though at a lower level of holiness than official priests, Aaron and his sons. The land of Canaan, the Land of Promise, is a holy land, which God has specially set apart for them (Lev. 25:23). All of this God ordained as a shadow or a prefigure of Christ, who was to come. He is the *Holy One* of God (Acts 3:14). By his work on the cross, our sins are forgiven and we become holy (1 Cor. 1:2). Christ is our righteousness (1 Cor. 1:30).

So just as there are distinctions and differences in treatment for holy places and holy foods in the Old Testament, there are distinctions between the church and the world. We are holy, while unbelievers are not. We treat fellow Christians as brothers and sisters in Christ, but we treat unbelievers only as neighbors. We endeavor to love them, because Christ told us to. But it is not the same brotherly love that we have for fellow Christians.

The bonds of fellowship are different inside and outside the church. This difference explains the necessity for excommunicating unrepentant sinners. First Corinthians 5 discusses in some detail a situation that included an unrepentant member of the Corinthian church. It indicates that the unrepentant man was to be put out of the church (vv. 5, 11). The passage differentiates pointedly between the treatment of outsiders and those within the Christian fellowship. Those within the fellowship are required to be holy in their conduct. If they are not and they do not repent, they must be expelled from the community, that is, from the church (excommunicated, 1 Cor. 5:5, 13). Members of the church must not continue to have Christian fellowship with them. On the other hand, Christians may mingle with unbelievers: "For what have I to do with judging outsiders?" the apostle Paul asks (1 Cor. 5:12).

Does all this mean that Christ is Lord only inside the holiness of the church? Of course not. Christ *saves* only those who are believers. He *rules* over all things, as we have already seen. He rules over the holy and the common, over the sacred and the profane.

Does this mean that we have an obligation to be holy *only* when we are assembled in church? Of course not. "But as he who called you is holy, you also be holy *in all your conduct*, since it is written, 'You shall be *holy*, for I am holy'" (1 Pet. 1:15–16).

But how can we be holy when we mingle with unbelievers? We are holy through the presence of the Holy Spirit, who permanently consecrates us and permanently indwells us. He empowers us to serve Christ in every circumstance. Thus, the distinction between holiness and commonness reinforces our motivation to serve Christ *in all of life*—"in all your conduct," as 1 Peter 1:15

says. We are distinct from and different from the world, even when physically we are surrounded by unbelievers and endeavor to co-operate with them in some task. Because God has made us holy, we should be serving Christ, even if others are not. And if the task involves sin, we cannot cooperate in it.

MINGLING WITH NON-CHRISTIANS

Let us consider a little further what happens when we as Christians mingle with non-Christians. We mingle because Christ instructs us to do so in 1 Corinthians 5. We are not made unclean or unholy by physical proximity to non-Christians, because the Holy Spirit dwells in us, makes us holy, and fills us with the power of Christ's indestructible resurrection life of holiness. When we serve Christ faithfully, we spread our holy behavior and holy thinking in the midst of the world, rather than being overcome by the world.

To put it another way, we mingle with non-Christians not because we are *like* them but precisely because we are so *unlike* them. At a deep level, we do *not* have common purposes. *Our* purpose is to glorify God by serving Christ; *their* purpose is to serve themselves or some idol. At a deep level, we do not have a common consciousness. *We* are conscious of the presence of God in us and in the display of his glory in the world that he has made; *non-Christians* are not (they have suppressed it, Rom. 1:18–23). We mingle with non-Christians not because at a deep level we have common purposes or common consciousness, but because of our Christian understanding of our holiness. By the power of Christ and by the indwelling of the Holy Spirit, God maintains our holiness even when we are physically close to the world.

At a deep level, Christians and non-Christians have antithetical purposes. So how can there be cooperation? I have earlier talked about common grace, and it is worthwhile to remember the principle of common grace again at this point. We can learn a lot from unbelievers. And we can cooperate with them in many cultural projects, whether in business or in economic transactions or in citizenship. But we have these shared projects in spite of, not because of, the direction of their hearts.

We should be thanking God for his goodness, which is repeatedly displayed in the good ideas and good deeds of unbelievers. We can praise the unbelievers themselves, admiring them and commending them for what God has given them and what he has worked through them. There is always room for a lot of genuine praise, rather than the kind of begrudging praise or even picky criticism that can characterize Christians who keenly sense the fundamental opposition between believing and unbelieving hearts. But this praise goes to God and to the gifts of God. It does not whitewash the state of unbelieving hearts or make unbelievers less rebels against God than they actually are. In fact, it makes their guilt more serious, because it is guilt in the context of all these good things that God is working in them.

We should also remember that we need wisdom in making decisions about our contacts with unbelievers. We live in the same larger society as they do. But which activities do we choose? Into which associations and relations do we enter? We have limited time: "Look carefully then how you walk, not as unwise but as wise, making the best use of the time, because the days are evil. Therefore do not be foolish, but understand what the will of the Lord is" (Eph. 5:15–17). We also need to avoid exposing ourselves to temptation. The person tempted by alcohol needs to avoid going out to a bar with his old drinking buddies. The same caution applies to any area of weakness.

We should note, finally, that though the unbelievers around us are not holy, they are religiously and morally obligated to bow to the lordship of Christ over all things. Their disobedience and their ignorance do not annul the reality of Christ's lordship.

HOLINESS SYMBOLIC AND REAL

For the sake of clarity about holiness, it is useful to stand back and look carefully at the big picture. The biblical theology of holiness spans the Old Testament and the New. The Old Testament uses shadows and images that point forward to the holiness of Christ and the holiness of God's people in the New Testament. It is wise to remember that the shadows in the Old Testament are indeed shadows, not the reality. For example, Leviticus 21 contains instructions for maintaining the outward holiness of the priests themselves. Leviticus 22 contains instructions for the holy food and holy offerings. Both kinds of holiness are *symbolic*. God forbids the priests in most circumstances from becoming unclean by touching a dead body (Lev. 21:1). If someone has a physical blemish, he is disqualified from being a priest (Lev. 21:17). These regulations offer symbols of the greater holiness still to come. Hebrews explains the difference between symbolic holiness and real holiness:

> By this [instructions about the tabernacle] the Holy Spirit indicates that the way into the holy places is not yet opened as long as the first section is still standing (which is *symbolic* for the present age). According to this arrangement, gifts and sacrifices are offered that cannot perfect the conscience of the worshiper, but deal only with food and drink and various washings, regulations for the body imposed until the time of reformation. But when Christ appeared as a high priest of the good things that have come, then through the greater and more perfect tent (not made with hands, that is, *not of this creation*) he entered once for all into the holy places, not by means of the blood of goats and calves but by means of his own blood, thus securing an eternal redemption. (Heb. 9:8–12)

The Old Testament priesthood is a symbol for Christ's priesthood. And, subordinately, it is a symbol for Christian priesthood, because all Christians are priests through the consecration that they receive from Christ.

> You yourselves like living stones are being built up as a spiritual house, to be *a holy priesthood*. (1 Pet. 2:5)

But you are a chosen race, a royal *priesthood*, a holy nation. (1 Pet. 2:9)

A similar principle of foreshadowing holds true for the holy food in Leviticus 22. It is symbolic of the holiness that is to come later. The food is holy because it is taken from the holy offerings that have been dedicated from the people of Israel. What does this holy food symbolize? The New Testament indicates that Christ is not only the High Priest but also the offering: "He has no need, like those high priests, to offer sacrifices daily, first for his own sins and then for those of the people, since he did this once for all when *he offered up himself*" (Heb. 7:27). Thus, the Old Testament holy food points forward to Christ. Subordinately, it also points forward to Christians, because they are united to Christ. Christians are to offer their own "bodies as a living *sacrifice*" (Rom. 12:1).

There is still another form of symbolic holiness in the Old Testament. The nation of Israel as a whole is called "a holy nation" (Ex. 19:6). It is a shadow of the people of God in the New Testament, whom God now calls "a holy nation" (1 Pet. 2:9).

Because the holiness of priests, of foods, and of the nation of Israel as a whole is only symbolic, each is superseded by the *real* holiness in the New Testament. That is why we no longer literally keep the instructions in Leviticus 21–22. That is also why we need not become Jews to obtain the special privileges of holiness that they had in the Old Testament (Gal. 3:28–29).

The relationship between symbolic holiness in the Old Testament and the real holiness in the New Testament is a relationship of analogy, not identity. The fullness belongs to Christ. Everything before Christ was a shadow. People in the Old Testament were spiritually nourished beforehand through the presence of Christ in his grace. But the ordinances that God put in place were external symbols rather than the reality.

Thus, we must be careful not to try to deduce all the meaning and implications of Christian holiness from Old Testament symbolism alone. The New Testament has something to say. Christ is the fullness of holiness. And since he is, his presence in New Testament fullness gives us richer and deeper insight into our present status of holiness.

How do these observations contribute to understanding Christian service to Christ in all of life? First Peter 1:15–16 is decisive, as we already observed: "But as he who called you is holy, you also be holy in *all your conduct*, since it is written, 'You shall be holy, for I am holy.'" It says "all your conduct," including not merely conduct "in church," but every day of the week.

The Mosaic law in the Old Testament distinguished holy spaces like the tabernacle from common spaces (in particular, the lands beyond the Promised Land). But the coming of Christ has transfigured and deepened the meaning of holy space. The Herodian temple in Jerusalem is no longer a holy space—in fact, it was destroyed in AD 70. Christ is the "holy space." And we who are in Christ are holy. No geographical location on earth is holy in and of itself. The church as a community is holy. In addition, our bodies are holy—the temple of the Holy Spirit. So the demands of Christ's holiness extend to all of life. Abraham Kuyper was right in stressing the implications of Christ's lordship for all of life.

The civil government or a Christian business or a musical group never becomes identical with the church and its holiness. The church is unique, by appointment of God. But whenever Christians function as agents of the state or of a business, they are still Christians. They are still holy. They should still be holy in their conduct. And that means that they "observe all that I [Jesus] have commanded you" (Matt. 28:20). In this obedience, Christians ought obviously to respect that Christ in his universal lordship has appointed each institution to have its own authority, as Abraham Kuyper emphasized. But through Christian obedience, all institutions in which they serve may be transformed.

Positive Summary

Many of the distinctions above, though they may be associated with two kingdoms theology, are useful for everyone and are positively relevant to our calling to serve Christ as Lord in all of life. Far from undermining the conviction that Christ is Lord, they support it. The distinctions just have to be properly understood.

For further discussion of these issues, I refer readers to John Frame's book *The Doctrine of the Christian Life*.[19] When we study Scripture and try to work out the principles for obedience to God, it becomes clear in a detailed way that scriptural instruction has implications for all of life, and that our responsibilities extend to all of life, not merely to some one aspect or some one ("holy") sphere.

Viable Bipolar Alternatives?

What about possible alternatives to the position I have set forth in this book?

We can continue to read about and investigate ongoing disputes over just how to conceptualize the relationship between church and state, and between the holy and the common. Related disputes arise in discussing the relationship between the influence of common grace and the influence of special grace, and between moral principles in general revelation ("natural law") and in special revelation. We can learn much from others, even from non-Christians, by virtue of common grace. But all ideas, from whatever source, including our own, must be critically inspected in the light of scriptural teaching, the only text with divine authority. General revelation too has divine authority, though not as a text, and not as "the power of God for salvation" (Rom. 1:16); its contents are distorted by sinful human reception that must be overcome by the Word and the Spirit.

---

[19] John M. Frame, *The Doctrine of the Christian Life* (Phillipsburg, NJ: P&R, 2008). In appendices E and F, Frame explicitly addresses some issues that have arisen in connection with writings representing two kingdoms theology.

As I have tried to make clear, Scripture itself indicates that all people know God and his moral standards (Rom. 1:18–23, 32), even if they have no contact with the Bible. The civil government has responsibilities to enforce justice, whether or not the officers of government consciously recognize that their responsibilities are ordained by God and have their source in God's character. No problem arises merely from recognizing such truths. In fact, they are part of the foundation for a biblical philosophy of government.

The danger arises if we artificially polarize two spheres—for example, a so-called secular sphere and a religious sphere. Or we polarize two sources of moral knowledge and act as though general revelation of moral standards can function well without the illumination and specific teaching of special revelation.

Some Christians have talked in a manner that does not intend such a polarization but nevertheless is misunderstood by some readers to imply polarization. It is easy to introduce polarization unconsciously because of modern social contexts. People who live in so-called modern societies commonly make assumptions that *do* polarize a realm of the secular, where God is allegedly absent, from a realm of the sacred, where it is allowed that he might be present, at least in the subjective minds of those who believe in him. So people think that science and art and business are "secular" and unrelated to God, but, if you feel like it, you can also participate in the "sacred" realm by praying to God in church or in the privacy of your home.

These polarizations cannot succeed. Christ is Lord of all. The polarizations are not only untrue to Christ, and untrue to reality, but also beset with internal paradoxes. Let us briefly consider the paradoxes in three different kinds of approaches.

Non-Christians who leave God out. One kind of approach comes from non-Christians who leave God out in their discussions. For these people, the central paradox is this. On the one hand, they usually do believe in *some* kind of moral basis for society. Otherwise, society could not survive and would disintegrate into mere barbarism and the power of the strongest. On the other hand, by eliminating God from the sphere of public morality, they leave no basis for why there are moral standards and why the standards are what they are.

Non-Christians who appeal to God as a source for moral standards. Other non-Christians appeal to God or gods as the source for morality. Adherents to other religions, such as Islam, Judaism, or Greek polytheism, may make such appeals. But then the question is What kind of God really exists? Is he a God who requires child sacrifice, or who requires people to practice jihad against infidels? The twisted sense of morality in some religions confirms the truth of the principle that conscience among fallen human beings is an uncertain guide.

Christians who appeal to a general sense of sanity and what is right. Some Christians may make only a minimal use of the Bible in arguments about Christianity and culture, church and state. They usually appeal to historical wisdom from Christians of previous generations. Or they appeal to analyses of the character of modern social structures. Or they invoke our general sanity and our sense of what is right. This last appeal is like an appeal to natural law. There may be much wisdom and insight contained in what they say, just as there is much wisdom and insight among non-Christians by virtue of common grace. But their appeals still need to be sifted in the light of Scripture.

We come back to the same point that we have made before: Scripture has divine authority. Facts of history, or facts about social structures, or even facts about what Christian people believed in previous generations do not lead directly to moral principles.[20] A movement from facts directly to moral principles contains a fallacy, the so-called naturalistic fallacy, which confuses what *is* with what *ought to be*.

---

[20] So also Klaas Schilder, *Christ and Culture*, trans. G. van Rongen and W. Helder (Winnipeg: Premier, 1977), 15; online with different pagination, accessed February 6, 2015, http://www.reformed .org/webfiles/cc/christ_and_culture.pdf, 19.

There is still one source for moral standards apart from Scripture, namely, natural law. Indeed, but everything depends on what we mean by natural law. If we mean whatever fallen human reason *postulates* as moral standards, we have no sound basis for morality. Apart from Scripture and renewal through the Holy Spirit, as sinful creatures we remain unaware of all the subtle ways in which sin corrupts our understanding of God and of his standards. Does natural law mean the general revelation of God's moral character through human conscience? Very well. But our consciences are corrupted by sin. A single simple argument from Scripture has greater claim to our allegiance than a hundred sophisticated appeals to our conscience. Among fallen humanity, conscience, by itself, boils down to each person's opinion about what he or she would like moral standards to be. It does not give us the stability of a well-founded standard.

Response. In response to these attempts to polarize realms or sources of morality, I would say, "Give it up." Recognize instead that Christ is Lord of all of life. Recognize that the Bible as the word of Christ speaks directly or indirectly concerning every sphere of life. When we become disciples of Christ, he liberates us from sin. In doing so, he liberates us also from compromises in allegiance and half-way measures and subservience to merely human opinion. Christ's voice is absolute. The voice of conscience is not.

The Calling of a Christian

Let us use God's instruction with care and submission. That instruction will itself lead us to be servants of Christ in every sphere. The Bible itself instructs us that when we are servants of Christ, we will love our neighbors and explore with sensitivity their situations, including the distinctive responsibilities that belong to different people, whether statesmen, lawmakers, workers, educators, students, church elders, husbands, wives, fathers, mothers, children, and so on.

We *will* build bridges to have relationships in certain specific ways with other people in family life, in politics, in church, and in work. But we will do so, not because our fundamental *allegiance* is compromised or divided, but because the love of Christ himself teaches us how to come alongside other people, acknowledging our own sin and fallibility, patiently bearing with others, and forgiving their sins when they ask. In this sense, the most mature and sanctified Christian should also be the gentlest and most flexible in human relationships. He is so precisely because Christ as absolute Lord and Redeemer, with all authority in heaven and on earth (Matt. 28:18), liberates him, commands him, guides him, and empowers him with the power and grace of the cross and the resurrection.

At the same time, this same Christian does not compromise *moral standards* or truth about God. He must always "obey God rather than men" (Acts 5:29).

Bibliography

Adam, Peter. *Hearing God's Words: Exploring Biblical Spirituality*. Downers Grove, IL: InterVarsity Press, 2004.

Ashford, Bruce Riley. *Every Square Inch: An Introduction to Cultural Engagement for Christians*. Bellingham, WA: Lexham, 2015.

Augustine. *The City of God*. In *A Select Library of the Nicene and Post-Nicene Fathers of the Christian Church*. Edited by Philip Schaff. Vol. 2. Grand Rapids, MI: Eerdmans, 1979.

Bahnsen, Greg L. *Van Til's Apologetic: Readings and Analysis*. Phillipsburg, NJ: P&R, 1998.

Bartholomew, Craig G., and Michael W. Goheen. *The Drama of Scripture: Finding Our Place in the Biblical Story*. Grand Rapids, MI: Baker Academic, 2004.

———. *The True Story of the Whole World: Finding Your Place in the Biblical Drama*. Grand Rapids, MI: Faith Alive Christian Resources, 2009.

Beale, G. K. *The Book of Revelation: A Commentary on the Greek Text*. Grand Rapids, MI: Eerdmans, 1999.

Bratt, James D., ed. *Abraham Kuyper: A Centennial Reader*. Grand Rapids, MI: Eerdmans, 1998.

———. *Abraham Kuyper: Modern Calvinist, Christian Democrat*. Grand Rapids, MI: Eerdmans, 2013.

Calvin, John. *Institutes of the Christian Religion*. Translated by Henry Beveridge. Grand Rapids, MI: Eerdmans, 1970.

Carson, D. A. *Christ and Culture Revisited*. Grand Rapids, MI: Eerdmans, 2008.

de Bruijn, Jan. *Abraham Kuyper: A Pictorial Biography*. Grand Rapids, MI: Eerdmans, 2014.

de Graaf, Simon G. "Christ and the Magistrate." Translated by Nelson D. Kloosterman. In *Kingdoms Apart: Engaging the Two Kingdoms Perspective*, edited by Ryan C. McIlhenny, 95–109. Phillipsburg, NJ: P&R, 2012.

Dennison, William D. "The Christian Academy: Antithesis, Common Grace, and Plato's View of the Soul." *Journal of the Evangelical Theological Society* 54, no. 1 (2011): 109–31.

———. "Dutch Neo-Calvinism and the Roots of Transformation." *Journal of the Evangelical Theological Society* 42, no. 2 (1999): 271–91.

———. "Review of VanDrunen's *Natural Law and the Two Kingdoms*." *Westminster Theological Journal* 75, no. 2 (2013): 349–70.

———. "Van Til and Common Grace." *Mid-America Journal of Theology* 9 (1993): 225–47.

Forster, Greg. *Joy for the World: How Christianity Lost Its Cultural Influence and Can Begin Rebuilding It.* Wheaton, IL: Crossway, 2014.

Frame, John M. *Apologetics: A Justification of Christian Belief.* 2nd ed. Phillipsburg, NJ: P&R, 2015. This is a revision of the 1994 volume *Apologetics to the Glory of God.*

———. "Christianity and Culture: Lectures Given at the Pensacola Theological Institute, July 23–27, 2001." Accessed February 9, 2015. http://www.thirdmill.org/new files/joh_frame/Frame.Apologetics2004.ChristandCulture.pdf.

———. *Cornelius Van Til: An Analysis of His Thought.* Phillipsburg, NJ: P&R, 1995.

———. *The Doctrine of God.* Phillipsburg, NJ: P&R, 2002.

———. *The Doctrine of the Christian Life.* Phillipsburg, NJ: P&R, 2008.

———. *The Doctrine of the Knowledge of God.* Phillipsburg, NJ: Presbyterian and Reformed, 1987.

———. *The Doctrine of the Word of God.* Phillipsburg, NJ: P&R, 2010.

———. *The Escondido Theology.* Lakeland, FL: Whitefield Media Productions, 2011.

———. *A History of Western Philosophy and Theology.* Phillipsburg, NJ: P&R, 2015.

———. *Perspectives on the Word of God: An Introduction to Christian Ethics.* Eugene, OR: Wipf & Stock, 1999.

———. "A Primer on Perspectivalism," 2008. Accessed July 14, 2014, http://www .frame-poythress.org/a-primer-on-perspectivalism/.

———. "Review of David VanDrunen's *A Biblical Case for Natural Law.*" Accessed September 29, 2014. http://www.frame-poythress.org/review-of-david-van -drunens-a-biblical-case-for-natural-law/.

Frame, John M., and Leonard Coppes. *The Amsterdam Philosophy: A Preliminary Critique.* Phillipsburg, NJ: Harmony, 1972.

Free Merriam-Webster Dictionary, online. http://www.merriam-webster.com /dictionary/vocation.

Geehan, E. R., ed. *Jerusalem and Athens: Critical Discussions on the Theology and Apologetics of Cornelius Van Til.* Nutley, NJ: Presbyterian and Reformed, 1971.

Goheen, Michael W. *A Light to the Nations: The Missional Church and the Biblical Story.* Grand Rapids, MI: Baker Academic, 2011.

Goheen, Michael W., and Craig G. Bartholomew. *Living at the Crossroads: An Introduction to Christian Worldview.* Grand Rapids, MI: Baker Academic, 2008.

Hart, D. G. *A Secular Faith: Why Christianity Favors the Separation of Church and State.* Chicago: Dee, 2006.

Heslam, Peter S. *Creating a Christian Worldview: Abraham Kuyper's Lectures on Calvinism.* Grand Rapids, MI: Eerdmans, 1998.

Hoch, Ronald E., and David P. Smith. *Old School, New Clothes: The Cultural Blindness of Christian Education.* Eugene, OR: Wipf & Stock, 2011.

Horton, Michael. *The Gospel Commission: Recovering God's Strategy for Making Disciples.* Grand Rapids, MI: Baker, 2011.

Hughes, John J., ed. *Speaking the Truth in Love: The Theology of John M. Frame.* Phillipsburg, NJ: P&R, 2009.

Kalsbeek, L. *Contours of a Christian Philosophy: An Introduction to Herman Dooyeweerd's Thought.* Edited by Bernard and Josina Zylstra. Toronto: Wedge, 1975.

Keller, Timothy. *The Reason for God: Belief in an Age of Skepticism.* New York: Dutton, 2008.

Kline, Meredith G. *Images of the Spirit* Grand Rapids, MI: Baker, 1980.

Kruger, Michael J. *Canon Revisited: Establishing the Origins and Authority of the New Testament Books.* Wheaton, IL: Crossway, 2012.

Kuyper, Abraham. *Lectures on Calvinism: Six Lectures Delivered at Princeton University under Auspices of the L. P. Stone Foundation.* Grand Rapids, MI: Eerdmans, 1931.

———. *Principles of Sacred Theology.* Translated by J. Hendrik de Vries. Grand Rapids, MI: Eerdmans, 1968.

———. "Sphere Sovereignty." In *Abraham Kuyper: A Centennial Reader,* edited by James D. Bratt, 463–90. Grand Rapids, MI: Eerdmans, 1998.

MacDonald, James, ed. *Christ-Centered Biblical Counseling.* Eugene, OR: Harvest House, 2013.

Machen, J. Gresham. *Christianity and Liberalism.* Grand Rapids, MI: Eerdmans, 2009. First published 1923 by Macmillan.

Martin, Linette. *Hans Rookmaaker: A Biography.* Downers Grove, IL: InterVarsity Press, 1979.

Mathison, Keith. "2K or Not 2K? That Is the Question: A Review of David Van-Drunen's Living in God's Two Kingdoms." Ligonier Ministries, December 9, 2010. http://www.ligonier.org/blog/2k-or-not-2k-question-review-david-vandrunens -living-gods-two-kingdoms/.

McCartney, Dan. "Ecce Homo: The Coming of the Kingdom as the Restoration of Human Vicegerency." *Westminster Theological Journal* 56, no. 1 (1994): 1–21.

McGoldrick, James Edward. *God's Renaissance Man: The Life and Work of Abraham Kuyper.* Darlington, UK: Evangelical Press, 2000.

McIlhenny, Ryan C., ed. *Kingdoms Apart: Engaging the Two Kingdoms Perspective.* Phillipsburg, NJ: P&R, 2012.

Mininger, Marcus. "Eschatology and Protology, Christ and Culture: Marriage as a Biblical Test-Case." *Mid-America Journal of Theology* 25 (2014): 117–40.

Mouw, Richard J. *Abraham Kuyper: A Short and Personal Introduction.* Grand Rapids, MI: Eerdmans, 2011.

Murray, John. "The Attestation of Scripture." In *The Infallible Word: A Symposium by Members of the Faculty of Westminster Theological Seminary.* Edited by N. B. Stonehouse and Paul Woolley, 1–54. 3rd ed. Philadelphia: Presbyterian and Reformed, 1967.

———. *Redemption Accomplished and Applied.* Grand Rapids, MI: Eerdmans, 1955.

Packer, J. I. *Knowing God.* Downers Grove, IL: InterVarsity Press, 1993.

Parler, Branson. "Two Cities or Two Kingdoms? The Importance of the Ultimate in Reformed Social Thought." In *Kingdoms Apart: Engaging the Two Kingdoms Perspective,* edited by Ryan C. McIlhenny, 173–97. Phillipsburg, NJ: P&R, 2012.

Plantinga, Cornelius, Jr. *Engaging God's World: A Christian Vision of Faith, Learning, and Living.* Grand Rapids, MI: Eerdmans, 2002.

Powlison, David. *The Biblical Counseling Movement: History and Context.* Greensboro, NC: New Growth, 2010.

———. *Seeing with New Eyes: Counseling and the Human Condition through the Lens of Scripture.* Phillipsburg, NJ: P&R, 2003.

Poythress, Vern S. "Counterfeiting in the Book of Revelation as a Perspective on Non-Christian Culture." *Journal of the Evangelical Theological Society* 40, no. 3 (1997): 411–18. Accessed December 4, 2014. http://www.frame-poythress .org/counterfeiting-in-the-book-of-revelation-as-a-perspective-on-non-christian -culture/.

———. "Indifferentism and Rigorism in the Church: With Implications for Baptizing Small Children." *Westminster Theological Journal* 59, no. 1 (1997): 13–29. Accessed July 9, 2014. http://www.frame-poythress.org/indifferentism-and-rigorism/.

———. *Inerrancy and the Gospels: A God-Centered Approach to the Challenges of Harmonization.* Wheaton, IL: Crossway, 2012.

———. *Inerrancy and Worldview: Answering Modern Challenges to the Bible.* Wheaton, IL: Crossway, 2012.

———. *In the Beginning Was the Word: Language—A God-Centered Approach.* Wheaton, IL: Crossway, 2006.

———. "Kinds of Biblical Theology." *Westminster Theological Journal* 70, no. 1 (2008): 129–42.

———. "Linking Small Children with Infants in the Theology of Baptizing." *Westminster Theological Journal* 59, no. 2 (1997): 143–58. Accessed July 9, 2014. http://www.frame-poythress.org/linking-small-children-with-infants-in-the-theology-of-baptizing/.

———. *Logic: A God-Centered Approach to the Foundation of Western Thought.* Wheaton, IL: Crossway, 2013.

———. "Multiperspectivalism and the Reformed Faith." In *Speaking the Truth in Love: The Theology of John M. Frame,* edited by John J. Hughes, 173–200. Phillipsburg, NJ: P&R, 2009. Accessed January 26, 2012. http://www.frame-poythress.org/poythress_articles/AMultiperspectivalism.pdf.

———. *Reading the Word of God in the Presence of God: A Handbook of Biblical Interpretation.* Wheaton, IL: Crossway, 2016.

———. *Redeeming Mathematics: A God-Centered Approach.* Wheaton, IL: Crossway, 2015.

———. *Redeeming Philosophy: A God-Centered Approach to the Big Questions.* Wheaton, IL: Crossway, 2014.

———. *Redeeming Science: A God-Centered Approach.* Wheaton, IL: Crossway, 2006.

———. *Redeeming Sociology: A God-Centered Approach.* Wheaton, IL: Crossway, 2009.

———. *The Returning King: A Guide to the Book of Revelation.* Phillipsburg, NJ: P&R, 2000.

———. "2 Thessalonians 1 Supports Amillennialism." *Journal of the Evangelical Theological Society* 37, no. 4 (1995): 529–38. Accessed May 11, 2015. http://www.frame-poythress.org/2-thessalonians-1-supports-amillennialism/.

———. *Symphonic Theology: The Validity of Multiple Perspectives in Theology.* Grand Rapids, MI: Zondervan, 1987. Reprint, Phillipsburg, NJ: P&R, 2001.

Rigney, Joe. *The Things of Earth: Treasuring God by Enjoying His Gifts.* Wheaton, IL: Crossway, 2014.

Rookmaaker, Hans R. *The Complete Works of Hans R. Rookmaaker.* Carlisle, PA: Piquant, 2003.

Sayers, Dorothy L. *The Mind of the Maker.* New York: Harcourt, Brace, 1941.

Schaeffer, Francis A. *The Complete Works of Francis A. Schaeffer: A Christian Worldview.* 5 vols. Wheaton, IL: Crossway, 1985.

Schilder, Klaas. *Christ and Culture.* Translated by G. van Rongen and W. Helder. Winnipeg: Premier, 1977. Accessed February 6, 2015. http://www.reformed.org/web files/cc/christ_and_culture.pdf.

Stapert, Calvin R. "To the Glory of God Alone." *Christian History* 95 (2007). Accessed September 20, 2014. http://www.christianitytoday.com/ch/2007/issue95/1.8.html.

Stonehouse, Ned. B., and Paul Woolley, eds. *The Infallible Word: A Symposium by Members of the Faculty of Westminster Theological Seminary.* 3rd ed. Philadelphia: Presbyterian and Reformed, 1967.

Storms, Sam. *One Thing: Developing a Passion for the Beauty of God.* Fearn, UK: Christian Focus, 2004.

Van Til, Cornelius. *Common Grace and the Gospel.* Nutley, NJ: Presbyterian and Reformed, 1972.

———. *The Defense of the Faith.* 4th ed. Edited by K. Scott Oliphint. Phillipsburg, NJ: P&R, 2008.

———. "Response by C. Van Til." In *Jerusalem and Athens: Critical Discussions on the Theology and Apologetics of Cornelius Van Til,* edited by E. R. Geehan, 89–127. Nutley, NJ: Presbyterian and Reformed, 1971. Here Van Til is responding to a chapter by Herman Dooyeweerd, "Cornelius Van Til and the Transcendental Critique of Theoretical Thought."

Van Til, Henry R. *The Calvinistic Concept of Culture.* Grand Rapids, MI: Baker, 1959.

VanDrunen, David. *A Biblical Case for Natural Law.* Grand Rapids, MI: Acton Institute, 2006.

———. *Divine Covenants and Moral Order: A Biblical Theology of Natural Law.* Grand Rapids, MI: Eerdmans, 2014.

———. *Living in God's Two Kingdoms: A Biblical Vision for Christianity and Culture.* Wheaton, IL: Crossway, 2010.

———. *Natural Law and the Two Kingdoms: A Study in the Development of Reformed Social Thought.* Grand Rapids, MI: Eerdmans, 2010.

Venema, Cornelis. "Christ's Kingship in All of Life: Butchers, Bakers, and Candlestick-Makers in the Service of Christ." *Mid-America Journal of Theology* 25 (2014): 1–27.

———. "One Kingdom or Two? An Evaluation of the 'Two Kingdoms' Doctrine as an Alternative to Neo-Calvinism." *Mid-America Journal of Theology* 23 (2012): 77–129.

———. *The Promise of the Future.* Carlisle, PA: Banner of Truth, 2000.

Vos, Geerhardus. *Biblical Theology: Old and New Testaments.* Carlisle, PA: Banner of Truth, 1975.

Warfield, Benjamin B. *The Inspiration and Authority of the Bible.* Edited by Samuel G. Craig. Philadelphia: Presbyterian and Reformed, 1967.

Westminster Confession of Faith. 1646.

Westminster Shorter Catechism. 1647.

Wittmer, Michael E. *Heaven Is a Place on Earth: Why Everything You Do Matters to God.* Grand Rapids, MI: Zondervan, 2004.

Wolters, Albert. *Creation Regained: Biblical Basics for a Reformational Worldview.* 2nd ed. Grand Rapids, MI: Eerdmans, 2005.

General Index

Scripture Index

Also Available from Vern Poythress

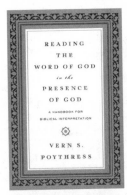

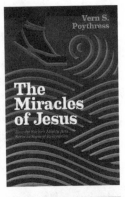

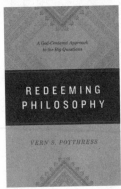